Kevin Miller
9/03

United Methodism

@RISK

A Wake-Up Call

Leon Howell

Study Guide by
Bishop C. Dale White and
The Rev. Scott Campbell

Information Project
for United Methodists
Kingston, New York

United Methodism @ **RISK:** A Wake-Up Call
Copyright©2003 by Information Project for United Methodists
All rights reserved.

Information Project for United Methodists
Kingston, New York • www.ipum.org after June 1, 2003
Manufactured in the United States of America

ISBN 0-615-12399-6

Additional copies of this book may be ordered from:
The Genesis III Group
P.O. Box 336
Deerfield, NH 03037
Toll-free phone: 888-829-2947
Fax: 603-463-5621
e-mail: genthree@genesisthree.com

Checks should be made out to "MMH Ventures."
Master Card and Visa accepted.

Cost of the book is $12.50 (includes shipping and handling).
Contact Genesis III for cost on multiple copies.

Contents

Part 2: Who Will Decide?

Part 3: A Wake-Up Call

About the Author

Writer and editor Leon Howell appears widely in the religious press. He is the author or editor of eight books and former editor of the journal, *Christianity and Crisis*. Howell spent four years in Singapore in the 1970s covering Asian church and society. The United Methodist Church was a participant in that project. *Southeast Asians Speak Out: Between Hope and Despair*, written with Barbara Howell, was the study book for the 1975 schools of Christian mission. *Funding the War of Ideas*, written in 1995, is reflected in Chapter 8 of this book.

Preface

Wake, Awake!

So begins the opening stanza of a great hymn. And so we begin our message to our brothers and sisters in The United Methodist Church.

Wake, Awake!

Our denomination is at great risk. The time to act is now. Organizations calling themselves "conservative renewal groups" are engaged in campaigns to change the essential nature of our church. They seek to take the church to a place where diversity and tolerance and breadth of spirit are in short supply. They look backwards to times when knowledge was feared, questioning was suppressed and imagination was squelched.

Groups like Good News, Renew, the Confessing Movement and the Coalition for United Methodist Accountability are working hand in hand with the Institute on Religion and Democracy to alter dramatically many aspects of United Methodist life and witness most of us hold dear.

Only now is the depth and scope of the threat emerging clearly. Those within the denomination who value and affirm diversity within the church have viewed these groups as simply having one perspective among many. They have trusted that all persons of good faith — liberal or conservative, evangelical or otherwise — must be part of the dialogue as we seek to understand God's truth and to manifest that in our daily living.

We can no longer afford to think in such terms. To continue to view "conservative renewal groups" as but one voice among others is naively to risk waking up in a vastly different church one day soon.

The ultimate goal of these groups is to control The United Methodist Church. Their strategy is to attain top leadership positions in the denomination. One tactic they use is spreading misleading and inflammatory charges about groups and individuals to United Methodists across the country. They indulge in character assassination and seek to drive the church apart by the use of wedge issues, calculated to cause dissension and division. Their desire is to impose not to dialogue.

These warnings sound dire, even sensationalized. They are not. Read the chapters that follow. You will find them validated.

Those involved in researching and writing this book have endeavored not to use the very tactics we deplore. We have made every effort to fairly and accurately to convey information. Even while exposing actions we believe destructive to our denomination, we have avoided personal attacks. That's why we sought Leon Howell, a prize-winning journalist of demonstrated fairness and with deep church roots, to tell the story.

The critiques contained within these pages use labels in so far as they are necessary to identify and distinguish. We are aware labels are misleading. Those involved in producing this book do not view it as a liberal response to conservatives. We, too, are evangelical. We believe we are compelled to give witness to the faith that is within us. We, too, are conservative. We seek to conserve the best of our denominational and national traditions. We, too, lay claim to the Good News that the God who was in Jesus Christ — the Christ who is the head of the Church — is calling us to affirm and celebrate the amazing diversity among people of faith.

We have seen clearly in these beginning years of the 21st century how, within the church, we replicate the polarizations outside the church. We turn against each other and fight each other, rather than being reconciled to and with each other. We believe that the God who was responsible for the creation, the One whose grace brought into being such a rich diversity of persons, expects more cooperation than con-

4

frontation from us.

We must answer important questions:

- How can we honor our differences of interpretation of Scripture, our distinctive theologies and our varying emphases for the mission of the church?
- Where is the will to blend our differences as a way to serve more faithfully the God who challenges and sustains us?
- How have we contributed to the grieving that God must do in response to our arrogance, self-righteousness and need to control?
- What might we learn from the compassionate Jesus who saw the presence of the Holy Spirit in all persons?

These are the questions that must shape our common life in The United Methodist Church.

We believe this document represents an act of faithfulness by persons who love God, who strive to follow Jesus, who have been transformed by the Christ of our faith. We hope it will stir people to act. We call upon those of you who share our convictions:

- To challenge persons related to "conservative renewal movements" within your annual conferences to respect the breadth of our United Methodist heritage.
- To ask those persons about the things recorded in these pages.
- To insist that those elected to General Conference have the good of the whole church as their goal.
- To hold our General Conference delegates accountable to approach that gathering with open minds and open hearts.
- To let delegates know you will be praying for them.

The United Methodist Church has a mission, a message and an opportunity to witness in this exceedingly complex time. We dare to believe that with trust and faith in God, our beloved denomination has a calling to fulfill.

The words of another great hymn inquire "Are ye able?"

We believe with the "guiding radiance" of Christ above, we indeed are able.

Acknowledgments

The Information Project for United Methodists wishes to express its deep appreciation to all those who have contributed to this study. We are particularly indebted to Hennepin Avenue United Methodist Church in Minneapolis, Minnesota, for its support and services graciously given as the fiscal sponsor of the project.

Numerous individuals have contributed their wisdom and experience to the study, including author Leon Howell, researcher Dr. Charlene Floyd, and contributing writers including Dr. Lewis C. Daly, Bishop C. Dale White, the Rev. Scott Campbell, the Rev. Kathryn Johnson and the Rev. Dr. Gilbert H. Caldwell.

This study would not have been possible without the support and personal contributions of the Project's Board and Advisory Committee.

Finally, the board expresses deep appreciation to all the United Methodist individuals who made significant sacrifices through their financial support of the study.

Board of Directors

Bishop C. Dale White and Beth Capen, Esq., Co-Presidents
The Rev. Taka Ishii, Vice President
The Rev. Philip C. Lawson, Secretary
Ms. Ruth Daugherty, Treasurer

Advisory Committee

Bishop Roy I. Sano, California
Ms. Peggy Billings, New York
The Rev. Dr. Gilbert H. Caldwell, Colorado
The Rev. John Carr, Connecticut
Ms. Dollie Watkins Crist, Florida
Ms. Dalila Cruz, Texas
The Rev. Kathryn Johnson, Washington, D.C.
The Hon. Gary G. Metoxen, Wisconsin
Ms. Marilyn J. Outslay, Oregon
The Rev. Jeanne Audrey Powers, Minnesota
The Rev. Dr. Tex Sample, Desert Southwest
The Rev. Dr. Traci West, New Jersey

Introduction

Begin with reality. The United Methodist Church — the source of joy for so many as the vessel of Good News, proclaiming salvation, grace and community — is inhabited by human beings and thus "falls short of the glory of God."

History teaches that members of churches have never dwelt in perfect harmony. Conflicts over ritual, belief, practice and behavior have been persistent.

Recall the debate between Paul and Peter in the early days of the Church. If Jesus was the fulfillment of the law, would converts be required to follow the Jewish law? Peter and the church in Jerusalem were largely Jews who leaned toward circumcision and strict observance of food laws (Acts 10:9ff). Paul — dealing with Roman converts — argued against food and circumcision requirements (Acts 15). Those who opted for maintaining the purity of the tradition and those who sought to address the message to shifting circumstances have both been in the Church from the beginning.

Some differences have developed into movements, often with distinct identities. Methodism — a vital reform movement within the Anglican tradition — was one of these. It has historically been more concerned about living out the Gospel in encounters with the world than in developing and enforcing theological conformity.

Even so, different perspectives have led to painful disagreements.

The early Methodist Church, divided on slavery and segregation, gave birth to many kinds of Methodists because of racial and theological reasons. In the 1940s, the church created the all-Black Central Jurisdiction. Provisional conferences have isolated Black and other racial ethnic Methodists structurally.[1]

Movements have arisen within The United Methodist Church that employ doctrine to exclude rather than include. Do you recognize who within the Methodist Church set the following goals:

• Eliminate unscriptural teaching from Methodist seminaries,
• Make the Sunday-school literature doctrinally sound,
• Open the press to conservative interests,
• Place evangelical books in the Course of Study, and
• Publish a monthly newspaper for the advancement of the historic Christian faith.[2]

Authors of these goals wanted to change the members of the Commission on the Methodist Course of Study for pastors who had not attended seminary. Their president called the Christology of many Methodist leaders inadequate. They accused some leaders, including bishops, of weakness, even heresy, on fundamentals of the faith as they defined them: the virgin birth, the atonement, the bodily resurrection.[3]

Sound contemporary? Actually it's a dip into the history of the Methodist League for Faith and Life, which flourished from 1925 into the 1930s. The league represented the Evangelical-Conservatives locked into battle with the Evangelical-Liberals after World War I. The league lost much of its energy with the arrival of The Great Depression and World War II.

Three-quarters of a century later, similar contention is under way in The United Methodist Church. Pressure is on to change United Methodist curriculum materials. Leaders are accused of flawed Christology, even heresy. Boards and agencies are under fire. Proposals to require leaders to conform to "classical Christianity" are circulating.[4]

The charges come from United Methodist organizations calling themselves *renewal* groups. Working together, they say they form a *conservative renewal movement.* The term *renewal* disturbs some observers who remember when it was used to describe progressive social-justice activity within the denomination. Similarly, some are disturbed by the name of the Confessing Movement, a conservative renewal group that borrows its name from the small portion of the German church that opposed Hitler. Significant numbers within the church believe the activities of these groups are destructive rather than renewing.

Those developing this book gave much thought to how to idenify the groups in these pages. Out of a sense of fairness and respect, this book will use the term they have chosen for themselves — conservative renewal groups.

An Affirmation

Those involved with this publication affirm the right of all United Methodists to participate in shaping the future of their church. We claim the strong and life-affirming term *evangelical*. It might be good if we could use evangelical-liberal and evangelical-conservative to designate our differences.

Twentieth century theologian Georgia Harkness called herself an "evangelical liberal." She was centered in Jesus Christ as she lived as a pacifist and activist for justice for all people.[5]

Voices of today — pacifists, social gospelers, people of color and people of differing sexual orientation — need to be heard. The United Methodist Church provides an understanding of the Church and the Gospel that encourages varieties of thoughtful faith and faithful action.[6]

More dialogue, not less, is required. We grow when challenged to see our limitations and errors. Only to point out the errors in the ways of others is to circumscribe the Spirit. We are diminished by our partial gospels.

An Orthodox priest from Kerala, India, put it well at a world mission conference in Melbourne in 1980:

> The Roman Catholic Church has its infallible Pope, the Protestants the infallible Bible, the Orthodox the infallible Tradition and hardly anyone has the full implication of the trinitarian faith.[7]

Concerns

Much of this book is devoted to looking at ways in which dialogue is being disrupted by the tactics — at times mean-spirited — of organizations claiming to speak for people in the pews. This book is not a blast at evangelicals. On the contrary, evangelicals will discover disruptive and harmful things being done in their name.

This book is a call to action. The next big test will come at the quadrennial United Methodist General Conference in April 2004 in Pittsburgh, Pennsylvania. General Conference petitions from conservative renewal groups — led by Good News and the Confessing Movement and backed by the Institute on Religion and Democracy — have potential to:

• Dramatically alter the church's social-justice ministry,
• Curtail the historic mission efforts of women,
• Threaten freedom of the pulpit and seminary classroom,
• Challenge the role of minorities, and
• Undercut the church's ability to support policies that renew the human community.

Good News and the Confessing Movement are well organized and funded. Good News received a $100,000 challenge grant toward General Conference efforts. A Good News supporter traveled for months recruiting people. Training is being offered to get people supportive of the conservative renewal groups' agenda elected as delegates to General Conference. Well-financed "war rooms" will mobilize those delegates in Pittsburgh — Good News brought 80 people to Cleveland in 2000. "Prayer warriors" will undergird them.[8]

These activities comply with the way the denomination does its work. Similarly, progressive United Methodists bring their energy, voice and resolutions to General Conference. To be heard in 2004, you need to know what this book shares:

• The broad agenda of conservative renewal groups,
• Major players in their activity and how they operate, and
• How their efforts can impact The United Methodist Church.

The Institute on Religion and Democracy (IRD) will be a key player. The institute was created and is sustained by right-wing secular foundations — about $4.4 million in IRD's first 20 years — to target progressive policies, people and structures within United Methodist, Presbyterian (USA) and Episcopal churches. IRD says it sends its *UMAction* newsletter free to 315,000 United Methodists, many of whom don't request it. The newsletter batters church leaders and institutions, structures and policies.

IRD's staff is small but the institute leverages its impact by working with conservative renewal groups within the three targeted churches. It thrives on exploiting wedge issues — subjects like abortion and homosexuality that incite emotional response.

IRD's attention to the 1993 ecumenical Re-Imagining Conference — which drew more than 2,000 women across denominational lines to discuss images of God emerging from women's study of Scripture and theology — is an example of a wedge issue. IRD continues to mischaracterize the conference and its speakers, making false claims of such things as goddess worship to alarm United Methodists.

Scott Field, director of legislative affairs for Good News, speaking at a recent conference sponsored by Good News and the Confessing Movement, encouraged the use of wedge issues to isolate opponents and build political alliances. Field proposed using wedge issues to discredit potential delegates to General Conference that do not meet criteria of the conservative renewal groups.[9]

United Methodist Bishop C. Joseph Sprague of the Chicago Episcopal Area is the latest target of opportunity for the conservative renewal movement. Sprague's challenge to the tenets of fundamentalism in a 2002 speech was the focus of 15 stories on him on the Good News website in mid-March 2003.[10]

Real people are chewed up in such attacks. They are called heretics, witches and troublers of the faithful. Freedoms and ministries are threatened, and congregations prevented from openly discussing matters of faith. Imaginative inquiry is squelched as an atmosphere of fear is created.

Stories of how people and congregations that have been attacked by conservative renewal groups in their efforts to gain political advantage are included in this book.

This book calls for a return to Wesleyan understandings of dialogue. Methodism founder John Wesley distinguished between essential and nonessential beliefs, calling nonessential beliefs "opinions." Mr. Wesley said:

> Though we cannot think alike, may we not love alike? May we not be of one heart, though we are not of one opinion? Without all doubt, we may. Herein all the children of God may unite, notwithstanding these smaller differences. These remaining as they are, they may forward one another in love and in good works.[11]

Endnotes

[1] *The Book of Discipline 2000* 14-20.
[2] McCutcheon 59-67.
[3] Ibid.
[4] Good News sample petitions for General Conference 2004.
[5] Skinner Keller.
[6] *The Book of Discipline 2000* 45-51.
[7] Howell *Acting in Faith* 11.
[8] Field "Confessing the Faith" Conference.
[9] Field and Heidinger, "Confessing the Faith" Conference.
[10] *Good News* website 23 March 2003 <www.goodnewsmag.org>.
[11] Wesley "Catholic Spirit."

Part 1
United Methodism at Risk

1
Cast of Characters

- Good News,
- Renew,
- The Mission Society for United Methodists,
- The Confessing Movement,
- Lifewatch,
- The Association for Church Renewal,
- A Foundation for Theological Education,
- Transforming Congregations, and
- Coalition for United Methodist Accountability.

What do these groups have in common? They are all part of the conservative renewal movement within The United Methodist Church. Steady growth has occurred in their numbers in recent years. They often work together and with the Institute on Religion and Democracy. (See Chapter 2.)

It can get confusing. The following descriptions can help.

Good News

Good News — the familiar name for A Forum for Scriptural Christianity within The United Methodist Church — was the first of the current-day conservative renewal groups within United Methodism. Few organizations have as clear a creation story.

Start in 1966 when Charles Keysor, pastor of Grace Methodist Church in Elgin, Illinois, had lunch with Jim Wall, editor of the *New Christian Advocate,* a magazine for Methodist clergy.

Keysor — who had been an editor of *Together,* a Methodist family magazine and later worked for the Arthur Anderson advertising agency in Chicago — had attended a Billy Graham Crusade Oct. 2, 1959, at age 35.[1] He went to seminary and was later ordained.

He and Wall agreed Keysor would write an article on evangelical concerns. His "Methodism's Silent Minority: A Voice for Orthodoxy" appeared in the *New Christian Advocate* of July 14, 1966. In it, Keysor argued that large numbers of orthodox Methodists who held "a traditional understanding of the Christian faith" had little or no representation in the "higher councils of the church."[2]

What is *orthodoxy?* Keysor said:

> We who are orthodox believe that the Christian faith is comprehensively declared in Holy Scripture and is succinctly summarized in the Apostle's Creed.

He pointed to five fundamentals he said shape the faith:
• Inspiration of Scripture,
• Virgin birth of Christ,
• Substitutionary atonement of Christ,
• Physical resurrection of Christ,
• Return of Christ.[3]

Keysor received about 200 positive responses. Encouraged, he published the first issue of *Good News* magazine from his parsonage basement in March 1967. It was mailed to 6,300 Methodists. His wife, Marge Keysor, suggested the name. The magazine quickly became the focal point for evangelicals hoping to change The United Methodist Church.[4]

Two months after *Good News* appeared, Keysor organized A Forum for Scriptural Christianity to engage in a variety of activities in the life of the church. In 1970, he joined the faculty of Asbury College in Wilmore, Kentucky, moving the enterprise with him.

Good News since has followed the direction set by Keysor, demanding change in the denomination and creating alternate institutions. The story was told on Good News' 30th anniversary in 1996 by James

V. Heidinger II, president of Good News. Following are several moments in the organization's history he noted:

- August 1970: 1,600 people registered for the first Good News national convocation in Dallas, Texas. Convocations have been held most summers since.
- 1975: At that year's convocation, Edmund W. Robb Jr. called for a more "Wesleyan" theological education for seminarians.
- 1977: A Foundation for Theological Education — headed in 2003 by Ed Robb III — was set up to fund training for professors in orthodox theology and to seek to place them in United Methodist seminaries.
- 1979: The Wesleyan Bristol Bible curriculum was first published.
- 1983: The Mission Society for United Methodists — see section that follows — was created to compete with the official mission program of the denomination.
- 1972: Good News took its first step into the General Conference legislative process. Since then, the group's efforts have increased with each General Conference. (See Chapter 9.)

In his 30-year review, Heidinger said evangelical activity had changed The United Methodist Church dramatically. He identified a dozen organizations formed during that time within and beyond the denomination. They include most of the groups discussed in this book:

- 1981: The Institute on Religion and Democracy;
- 1983: UM Action and the Mission Society for United Methodists; and
- 1994: The Confessing Movement.[5]

Keysor concluded his "Silent Majority" article with these words:
> We must not speak as right-wing fanatics, intending to subvert the 'establishment' and remake it in our own orthodox image. Instead, we must speak to our Christian brothers as Christian brothers, trusting that God will direct and prosper our witness to the truth as we see it in Christ Jesus our Lord.[6]

The Disconnect
Charles Keysor was right. Trouble begins when a small group tries to herd everyone in the church into its orthodox image. Keysor's critics charge that in his zeal to apply the fundamentals of faith as he saw

them, he often failed to speak to those with whom he disagreed as brothers and sisters in the faith. Critics say he blazed a harsh trail that shut out and too often defamed those with whom he contended, a precedent followed today by the Good News movement and its magazine.

Look at Keysor's response to the 1972 General Conference — the first at which Good News was officially present. He decried "women's theology, liberation theology, Black theology, Third World theology, theologies of human rights, etc. The primary accent is upon man's ideas and problems instead of God's truth."[7]

He saw no merit in talking to or learning from theological viewpoints other than his white U.S. male perspective.

And how to combat dilution of his fundamentals?

"You folks back home have in your checkbooks the final and decisive veto," Keysor wrote.[8]

In his 30th anniversary piece, Heidinger said the 1972 General Conference "was a disaster, approving abortion and adopting the statement on theological pluralism...."

Keysor's attacks on United Methodist theological opinions other than his own continued. In 1974, he wrote an editorial in *Good News* magazine, "Confronting the Cults," in which he named "humanism" as the most widespread cult within United Methodism. He said a common form of humanism was "minority mania — the preoccupation by the church with minorities which represent only a small fraction of the whole membership...."[9]

Keysor and Good News framed the "homosexual issue" in ways that alarmed many United Methodists. Good News mailed letters in 1974 to about 15,000 United Methodists urging them to oppose the ordination of gay men and lesbians. Included in that mailing was a reprint of Keysor's article, "The Gathering Storm." Recipients were asked to give copies to lay members of annual conferences. In the letter, he warned that a "powerful homosexual caucus" would pressure the next General Conference to open "the floodgates" by ruling that "homosexual practice" was not wrong.[10] No such caucus existed.[11]

In 1978, Good News opposed a world food reserve proposed — and secured — by Bread for the World, the bi-partisan Christian anti-hunger movement. Later Good News rejected the possibility "that we in the United States, who constitute 6 percent of the world's population, (are) somehow guilty because we consume 35 percent of the world's goods and services."[12]

Keysor and others in the Good News movement employ acid-laced rhetoric. For example, Keysor used Nazi imagery — "Gathering Storm," and *blitzkrieg* to describe advocacy for ethnic minorities and homosexual persons in United Methodist legislative settings.[13] Good News advocated for under-represented evangelicals but called presumptuous the same rights for under-represented minorities or women to pursue their agendas.

Good News has labeled those it opposes with terms of disease such as *leprosy* and *cancer*.[14] In 1971, Leslie Woodson, then chair of the Good News Board of Directors, commended those within the movement as "Leucocytes in the Body of Christ" — white blood cells fighting to reject an infection.[15]

After the 1980 General Conference, Keysor asked the Good News board if it was committed to working only within The United Methodist Church. When the board affirmed its intention to do so, Keysor resigned leaving in January 1981 to teach journalism full-time at Asbury College.

He later left The United Methodist Church. Heidinger succeeded him as the primary Good News voice.[16]

Good News continues in Keysor's crusader bent. For example, its leaders continue to distort and exploit the 1993 Re-Imagining Conference. Organized by an ecumenical group of volunteers to respond to the goals of the World Council of Churches' Ecumenical Decade: Churches in Solidarity with Women, the Re-Imagining Conference drew more than 2,000 people from around the world to consider images of God from women's biblical and theological study. Good News continues to claim that those at the conference engaged in goddess worship and endorsed heretical teachings — reports participants say are false.

Organizational details

Good News identifies its mission as follows:

> The Good News movement is a voice for repentance, an agent for reform, and a catalyst for renewal within The United Methodist Church. By God's grace, we proclaim and demonstrate the power and effectiveness of historic Christianity as emphasized in Wesleyan doctrine and practice.

Good News, which has never depended on foundation grants, had audited revenues of about $1.1 million each year from 1997-1999.[17] Controller Brad Lewallen said 2002 pre-audit revenues were about $950,000.

Good News magazine's paid circulation had dropped sharply by the 1990s. In a January 1995 fund-raising letter, Heidinger announced Good News was "taking a step of faith" to send the magazine free to thousands of United Methodists and United Methodist churches that year. Lewallen said *Good News* magazine is going free to about 40,000 recipients in 2003.

The Good News Board of Directors is self-perpetuating, not elected by the larger church as are the agency directors they criticize as unaccountable. There were 34 directors listed on the Good News website in April 2003, with close to 20 states represented. Seven of these directors are women. Three of the directors are:

- Mark Tooley, UM Action director for the Institute on Religion and Democracy;
- Bradley C. Knepp, pastor of Mount Holly Springs United Methodist Church in Mount Holly Springs, Pennsylvania, who joined 27 pastors and laity to bring charges against United Methodist Bishop C. Joseph Sprague, see page 113; and
- Janice Shaw Crouse, a speechwriter for the first President Bush and staff of the right-wing Beverly LaHaye Institute. Crouse has assisted Good News in writing petitions for annual conferences. Crouse has said, "Certain statements in *The Book of Discipline of The United Methodist Church, 2000* are contrary to Bible teaching and need to be revised."[18]

Good News structure

The staff of Good News includes:
- James V. Heidinger II, president and publisher;
- Steve Beard, editor;
- Brad Lewallen, controller; and
- Faye Short, president of Renew Women's Network.

The Good News website — www.goodnewsmag.org — says it links readers to "ministries offering the transforming power of Christ to a lost and dying world." The website includes links to:

- Transforming Congregations,
- Lifewatch,
- The Confessing Movement,
- Methodists United in Prayer,
- Association for Church Renewal, and
- The Mission Society for United Methodists.

Renew

In July 1989, Good News created Renew: A Network for Christian Women with a twofold purpose:

- To help women establish and maintain a relationship with Christ, and
- To renew the Women's Division of the United Methodist General Board of Global Ministries.[19]

Renew, headed by Faye Short and based in Cornelia, Georgia, began as the Evangelical Coalition for United Methodist Women. Calling supporters "Agents for Reform," Renew says it is organized to promote renewal and accountability within United Methodist Women. Its website says:[20]

> We seek to help our great church restore faithfulness to Scriptural Christianity, to United Methodist doctrinal standards, and to our Wesleyan heritage.

In anticipation of General Conference 2004, Renew launched a "Call for Reform" of United Methodist Women/Women's Division. The plan if implemented would dramatically change women's mission outreach within The United Methodist Church limiting women's voice and vote in decision-making and curtailing women's social-justice ministries. (See Chapter 4.)

Frequent mailings from Renew and its page in *Good News* magazine are often devoted to attacking the Women's Division — its staff and directors, resources and programs, vision and purpose. Accountability — a theme borrowed from Good News — is Renew's rallying cry. Renew's accountability structure is unclear. No directors are listed on its website and there is no indication it is more than a three-woman operation within the Good News organization.

Those on Renew's mailing list receive a monthly letter. Most contain a negative critique of the Women's Division and a request for money. As recently as February 2001, Renew was not self-supporting as revealed in a letter from Short:

> Within our 12 years of ministry, we have not reached the place where we have been able to pick up, from Good News, the cost of our staff salary expenses. Given the fact that we only have three persons on the Renew staff, this is a real disappointment to me. Renew is greatly blessed with a working committee, whose members volunteer hundreds of hours of time to assist us with the broad scope of our ministry...however, much of Renew's work is done directly from the Renew office by this small staff of three....Let's surprise the Good News Board of Directors with our ability to pay ALL of our expenses...[21]

Contrast this to United Methodist Women whose members support a $20 million-a-year mission program that impacts women, children and youth across the United States and around the world.

Renew's critique of the Women's Division is consistent. Take the division's spiritual-growth studies. Renew finds them "unbiblical." Two examples: the text for a study of the Book of James was described as "a study of Scripture entangled in socialist critique"[22] and a study on Corinthians as "steeped in a liberal bias that challenges the authority of Scripture."[23]

Renew's reviews of United Methodist Women's mission-study resources are filled with challenges to the role of social justice in mission:[24]

• On *Mexico: Labyrinth of Faith,* 2002-2004 study book, Renew said: "The study's heavy emphasis on social activism gives the impression that activism is the answer to Mexico's problems."
• On *Restorative Justice: Moving Beyond Punishment,* 2002-2003 study book: "I was taken aback by the strident political tone of much of (the book's) rhetoric."

Renew makes similar claims about United Methodist Women's *Response* magazine, its annual program book, schools of Christian mission, and other resources and events.

Renew's vision statement says:

> The vision of Renew is to participate in the process of lead-

ing the women of the church into a personal and vital relationship with Jesus Christ; to provide a firm scriptural foundation for discernment in their faith; and to encourage, equip and impassion them for discipleship and witness in family, church, community and world.[25]

Renew shares Good News' tactic of discrediting individuals. Short regularly criticizes Women's Division top staff person Joyce D. Sohl and calls out the names of specific staff people when attacking actions of the division.[26] This in contrast to Short's statement in the May-June 2002 *Good News* magazine:[27]

> (Renew's) call is biblically based and expressed in a context of respectful disagreement. Unfortunately, too often the debate has sunk to unfair and undocumented *ad hominem* attacks, which means "against the man." This takes place when attempts are made to discredit anyone who raises concerns — such as Renew, Good News and UM Action.

Renew offers women alternatives to Women's Division resources and activities:

• Programming materials, Bible studies and books to read produced by Good News/Renew, Bristol House Ltd. and other conservative renewal groups.
• Workshops and hospitality rooms at United Methodist Women's Assemblies.
• Previews of non-United Methodist Women's programs during luncheons in the Good News hospitality suite at the 2000 General Conference.
• Global Celebration for Women, an event for conservative renewal women held in September 2001 at the Houston, Texas Astrodome. About 10,000 women attended. Event planners, now known as Global Christian Women, name partners on their website — www.globalchristianwomen.org: Women Aglow, Campus Crusade for Christ-Women Today, Assemblies of God Women's Ministries, Southern Baptist Women's Missionary Union, and the Institute on Religion and Democracy.

Renew would have us believe they have wide support:

> We are receiving hundreds of requests for the "Call for Reform of the Women's Division" packet....These requests are coming by phone, letter, e-mail and through website access.[28]

Two examples suggest smaller numbers:

- A widely publicized Renew workshop at the 1998 United Methodist Women's Assembly drew about 20 women from close to 10,000 at the event.
- A Renew-sponsored luncheon to introduce an alternative women's program during General Conference 2000 drew a handful of people, most from the contingent of Good News supporters there to lobby the conference.

Renew's newsletters, website and other communications do not indicate the group has a board of directors. They do refer to an "Oversight Committee" currently chaired by Bradley C. Knepp, United Methodist pastor in Mount Holly Springs, Pennsylvania, who is a member of the Good News Board of Directors.

Information on Renew can be found on its website: www.renewnetwork.org.

The Mission Society for United Methodists

The Mission Society for United Methodists' mission statement is found on its website — www.msum.org:

> The Mission Society's passion is to make Jesus Christ known to people who have had little or no access to the Gospel. As such, our strategies vary according to the needs of the people. Our missionaries serve in areas of education, health care, economic and community development, literacy training, music, construction, discipleship, and church planting. Through all these efforts, they introduce the love and message of Jesus.[29]

The society was formed in 1984 by individuals concerned about reaching 1.7 billion people who have not heard the Gospel. Its goal is to "complete the task of world evangelization."

Among mission-society founders was Ira Gallaway, who currently is a member of the boards of directors of the society and the Institute on Religion and Democracy, and is assistant executive director of the Confessing Movement.

Creation of the society ended a decade of discussions between the United Methodist General Board of Global Ministries and the Evangelical Missions Council. Good News has said repeatedly that the General Board of Global Ministries, the official mission arm of The United

Methodist Church, is too involved in social change and not sufficiently committed to sending U.S. evangelists to other nations.

The Good News' critique comes in response to changing patterns of mission outreach. During the first half of the 20th century, United Methodism's predecessor denominations sent missionaries from the United States to start churches in Africa, Asia, Latin America and the Pacific Islands. Many of those churches have matured into independent entities that are in partnership with but autonomous from the U.S. church. The churches grew in part because they did their own evangelism.

In some parts of the world — like China and Indonesia — rapid church growth took place with few missionaries present.

Western missionary-sending agencies changed, becoming partners in mission. That means listening as well as talking. That implies churches' accepting missionaries from other countries to speak to our needs. It involved supporting a professor from Japan who was asked by the Thai church to teach in its seminary and sending an African woman doctor to Russia. Twenty years ago, it meant several mainline mission boards quietly buying a printing press for the China Christian Council, which has printed 30 million Bibles since. The General Board of Global Ministries through the years has put about $1 million into that effort. At the same time, conservative renewal groups got publicity by getting arrested for trying illegally to smuggle Bibles into China.[30]

Something of this was involved in the debates with — and accusations against — the General Board of Global Ministries. How best to fulfill the Great Commission deserves serious discussion. The fervor to win souls is understandable, but nothing in the mission society's public material suggests a holistic view of mission. It's about Americans going overseas.

The society's website says it has 151 missionaries assigned to 29 countries on five continents. Among the countries are France, Ghana, Tanzania, Russia, Kazakhstan, India, Japan, Philippines, Mexico, Costa Rica, Peru and Paraguay. The society also offers short-term volunteer mission experiences.

The society's website says its board of 30 volunteer directors includes clergy, laity and missiologists from throughout the United States. A staff of 30 administers the program from headquarters in Norcross, Georgia. The society's website says:

Individuals and local churches support the Mission Society and underwrite the support of our missionaries. The Mission Society is a member of the Evangelical Council for Financial Accountability, which annually monitors its finances. The Mission Society is also a member of the Evangelical Fellowship of Mission Agencies. It is supported entirely by the financial contributions of individuals and local churches.

Steven DuBose, chief financial officer for the society, said the society also receives funding from family foundations. The society has about 1,500 donors, half individuals and the majority of the rest United Methodist churches, DuBose said.

In 2001, the society had revenues of $6,681,369. In 2000, revenues were $6,517,994.[31]

Lifewatch: The Taskforce of United Methodists on Abortion and Sexuality

Lifewatch was formed by nine pastors and laypeople meeting in Washington, D.C., in August 1987. Its original name was the Taskforce of United Methodists on Abortion and Sexuality. It now uses the name Lifewatch and has a newsletter by the same name with a circulation of 4,000.

Administrator Ruth Brown said in a telephone interview from Dothan, Alabama, in March 2003 that its budget was about $30,000 a year. "Our members are those who share our mission," Brown said.

The March 2003 *Lifewatch* newsletter — available on-line at www.lifewatch.org — contains two sample anti-abortion petitions for annual conferences. The organization's website states its mission:

Out of obedience to Jesus Christ, the Taskforce of United Methodists on Abortion and Sexuality (TUMAS) works to create — in church and society — esteem for human life at its most vulnerable, specifically for the unborn child and for the woman who contemplates abortion. Therefore, TUMAS's goal is to win the hearts and minds of United Methodists, and to engage in abortion prevention through theological, pastoral, and social emphases that support human life.

The website goes on to say:

> TUMAS has worked within the annual conferences to educate United Methodists about the realities of abortion and to bring about change which both protects the life of the unborn child and honors the lifelong health and welfare of the woman facing a crisis pregnancy....Lifewatch receives no funds and little publicity from the denomination. We depend entirely on the prayers, donations, and personal involvement of like-minded individuals.

Following are excerpts from prayer suggestions on the website:

- "Pray that our United Methodist denomination, which is currently facing a major crisis, will reclaim its Biblical, orthodox roots."
- "Pray that God will raise up humble, wise, godly, pro-life United Methodists as delegates to upcoming General and Jurisdictional Conferences."
- "Pray that the United Methodist Church will break all ties with the Religious Coalition for Reproductive Choice."

Among Lifewatch advisory board members listed on the website are:

- Deceased United Methodist Bishop William R. Cannon;
- Stanley Hauerwas, professor of theological ethics at Duke Divinity School;
- John E. Juergensmeyer, attorney and professor at Judson College in Elgin, Illinois;
- Priscilla Lynd, a pediatrician from Lexington, Kentucky;
- Thomas C. Oden, professor of theology and ethics at Drew Theological School and chair of the Institute on Religion and Democracy;
- Paul T. Stallsworth, Lifewatch board president and pastor of St. Peter's United Methodist Church in Morehead City, N.C.; and
- Geoffrey Wainwright, professor of Christian theology at Duke University.

The Confessing Movement

The emergence of confessing movements among conservative renewal United Methodists in 1994-1995 and their counterparts in the Presbyterian Church (USA) in 2001 is a major development in mainline Protestant denominations. These movements claim to introduce a renewed theological focus to the Church. The result has been to escalate denominational controversies. The movement was launched at a 1994 invitation-only gathering of about 100 people. The meeting was convened by the late Bishop William R. Cannon; Maxie Dunnam, president of Asbury Theological Seminary; and Thomas C. Oden, a professor of theology and ethics at Drew Theological School and chair of the Institute on Religion and Democracy.

The Confessing Movement among United Methodists is explained on the movement's website — www.confessingumc.org:

> We are a movement within The United Methodist Church, inseparable from it, not apart from it. All of us intend to stay within it....The Confessing Movement is not asking for a new definition of faith, but for a new level of integrity in upholding our historic doctrinal standards in a thoughtful, serious, and principled way. We look to our Council of Bishops to assert their traditional doctrinal teaching authority.

The Confessional Statement of the movement claims:

> [W]e repudiate teachings and practices that misuse principles of inclusiveness and tolerance to distort the doctrine and discipline of the church....We deny the claim that the individual is free to decide what is true and what is false, what is good and what is evil.[32]

The movement claims a membership of more than 600,000 individuals, 1,416 member churches and 3,975 pastors.[33]

In September 2002, a group of theologians from seven denominations was convened in Dallas, Texas, by Oden. This group drafted a statement entitled: "Be Steadfast: A Letter to Confessing Christians," in which the authors urge confessing-movement members to stay in their denominations.[34]

A month later, approximately 700 members from some 12 conservative renewal movements gathered in Indianapolis for the "Confessing the Faith" Conference — the first such confessing-movement gathering across denominations. Those present approved the "Be Steadfast" statement. Signatories included individuals from the three denominations targeted by the Institute on Religion and Democracy — The United Methodist Church, The Presbyterian Church (USA) and the Episcopal Church (USA) — and the Evangelical Lutheran Church in America, the United Church of Christ, the American Baptist Church and the United Church of Canada.

The event took place under the auspices of the Association for Church Renewal, formed in 1996 to bring together conservative renewal groups from mainline Protestant denominations. Executives of these organizations have been meeting annually since 1979 to share ideas and strategies.

The "Be Steadfast" statement is one in a line of declarations and statements issued by the Confessing Movement and, before its formation, Good News. The 1975 Junaluska Declaration — named for the Lake Junaluska, North Carolina, meeting site — emerged from an conclave of Good News. It said:

> In a time of theological pluralism, Good News and other evangelicals within United Methodism have thought it necessary to reaffirm the historic faith of the Church.[35]

Although mild in tone compared to more recent declarations, this declaration laid the groundwork for theological conformity and rigid interpretations of the Bible. Among the signers were Good News founder Charles Keysor and current Good News President James V. Heidinger II.

At the Lake Junaluska meeting, Good News stalwart Edmund W. Robb Jr. declared United Methodism "sick," pointing a finger at the seminaries:

> Let us serve notice, here and now, that we will no longer turn over our converts to the theological liberals who neither understand or teach the Biblical faith. Let us serve notice that evangelicals will no longer be silent concerning the great issues of the church, and follow blindly their impotent policies. We are dedicated to evangelical renewal within the United Methodist Church. We are not going elsewhere. Rather, we propose to radically alter the direction of our great denomination. This will come with revival. The revival fires are spreading across the land. Its impact will organizationally and educationally change United Methodism.[36]

Robb founded A Foundation for Theological Education in 1977. (See page 33.) He is on the Asbury Theological Seminary Board of Directors.

The next document was the Houston Declaration issued in anticipation of the 1988 General Conference. Its authors: Good News leaders. The declaration focused on "the primacy of Scripture; the name and nature of the one God, Father, Son and Holy Spirit; and the high and holy character of ordained ministry."[37]

Our Theological Task adopted by the 1988 General Conference and found in the *Book of Discipline,* reflects the first concern. A section that explains the Wesleyan quadrilateral says, "Scripture is primary, revealing the Word of God."

> On the Trinity, the Houston Declaration said:
>> Formulas such as "Creator, Redeemer, Sustainer" or "Creator, Christ, Spirit," are inadequate substitutes. As to the first: God's richly personal being cannot be defined merely in functional terms. As to the second, Christ and the Spirit are not mere creatures.

Addressing ordained ministry, declaration signers focused on retaining the ban on ordination of homosexual persons. That ban stands today.

The 1992 Memphis Declaration came next. It received less attention than its 1987 cousin. It fleshed out the conservative renewal agenda on abortion and homosexuality:

> We challenge the Church to be unequivocal in support of the Christian family, the sanctity of human life, and Christian sexual morality: fidelity in marriage and celibacy in singleness."[38]

The declaration ignores Jesus' explicit prohibition against divorce on which there is much compromise among Christians.

The Confessing Movement emerged out of this history with Good News President Heidinger at the helm.

Many United Methodists were stunned by the choice of name. "Confessing Church" was the name selected at the Barmen conference of Germans, such as Dietrich Bonhoeffer, who risked their lives to resist the Nazis' demand that churches sign a loyalty oath to Hitler.

There have been repeated denials that the name is more than saying Christians confess certain beliefs, but Heidinger, in the June/July 1997 *Good News* magazine, suggested otherwise:

> James R. Edwards, a Presbyterian minister and professor at Jamestown College in Jamestown, North Dakota, finds im-

portant parallels between our mainline church crisis and the historic Barmen Declaration of 1934, which grew out of the "German church struggle" *(Theology Matters,* Jan/Feb 1997). Edwards describes two understandings of Christianity reflected in the German struggle. One, represented by the "German Christians," advocated a "positive Christianity" that sought to integrate the gospel as far as possible with the prevailing ideology ushered in by Hitler and National Socialism. They would have urged the church to adapt to the new thought of the day. The other understanding was expressed by the "Confessing Church," which at Barmen and subsequent synods raised a voice of protest against reformulating Christianity according to Germanic and especially Nazi archetypes.

The lessons to be learned from Barmen are applicable for the mainline churches today, says Edwards, for our struggle is (like theirs) "over the authority of Scripture and creed versus the authority of the alien and humanistic ideologies, between the church's faithfulness to the Lordship of Christ as he is attested to in Scripture versus an accommodation and reformulation of Christianity to the spirit of the age....

...We criticize the German Christians for their accommodation to Hitler. However, we forget that they were simply accommodating Christian thought to the prevailing cultural norms of their day. And we are doing the same thing today....[39]

This parroting of the Barmen Declaration and smearing of faithful United Methodists as akin to Nazis was compounded when declaration authors asked all United Methodists to sign the "Confessing Church Declaration." A loyalty oath with rigid interpretations of Scripture and the United Methodist doctrinal heritage was dressed up as resistance to an evil force in the denomination.

Patricia Miller is executive director of the Confessing Movement; Ira Gallaway is the assistant executive director. Miller is a state senator in Indiana. Gallaway is former general secretary of the General Board of Evangelism (now part of the General Board of Discipleship), former chair of the Asbury Theological Seminary Board of Trustees and former chair of the board of the Mission Society for United Methodists.

The Association for Church Renewal

Association for Church Renewal Chair James V. Heidinger II, who is also president of Good News, said the association was formed in 1996 to institutionalize a network of conservative renewal groups and individuals to address common concerns, including: "moral relativism, marriage and family, human sexuality, neo-pagan worship, God-language, the free exercise of religion at home and abroad, the sanctity of life, and world mission and evangelism."[40]

Association members share strategies and resources toward promoting their concepts of orthodox leadership in mainline Protestant churches. Heidinger said association-linked publications reach an estimated 2.4 million people. This figure could not be confirmed.[41] Member groups of the Association for Church Renewal follow:

• Alliance for Confessing Evangelicals;
• American Anglican Council;
• American Baptist Evangelicals, American Baptist Church;
• American Lutheran Publicity Bureau, Evangelical Lutheran Church in America;
• Biblical Witness Fellowship, United Church of Christ;
• Community of Concern, United Church of Canada;
• Disciple Renewal, Disciples of Christ;
• Episcopalians United, Episcopal Church, USA;
• Evangelical Lutheran Confessing Fellowship, Evangelical Lutheran Church in America;
• Good News, The United Methodist Church;
• The Institute on Religion and Democracy;
• National Alliance of Covenanting Congregations;
• Presbyterian Layman, Presbyterian Church (USA);
• Presbyterians for Faith, Family and Ministry, Presbyterian Church (USA);
• Presbyterians for Renewal, Presbyterian Church (USA);
• Presbyterians Pro-Life, Presbyterian Church (USA);
• Renew Women's Network, The United Methodist Church;
• The Confessing Movement, The United Methodist Church;
• The Renewal Fellowship, The United Methodist Church;
• Transforming Congregations, The United Methodist Church; and
• Word Alone, Evangelical Lutheran Church in America.

A Foundation for Theological Education

A Foundation for Theological Education provides scholarships for doctoral work in theological education. Created in 1977, the foundation was the idea of Edmund W. Robb Jr., first president of the Institute on Religion and Democracy and long-time Good News stalwart. Foundation leaders work to place those who share their beliefs into teaching posts at seminaries and universities.

According to *Catalyst* (http://catalystresources.org) — a quarterly publication of the foundation that goes to 5,000 seminary students a year — more than 100 students have received scholarships, which are called John Wesley Fellowships. Five students annually receive $10,000 each for up to four years. Sixty-nine recipients have received PhD's and 40 are teaching at theological seminaries, including Duke, Wesley, Asbury, Dubuque, Princeton, Garrett-Evangelical and Perkins. The president of Garrett-Evangelical Theological Seminary is a John Wesley Fellow.[42]

The foundation had assets of $1,672,178 and income of $253,948 in 2000.[43]

Transforming Congregations Movement

The Transforming Congregations Movement recruits local congregations to adopt its understanding of homosexual practice as a sin from which people can be healed. Member churches are encouraged to establish programs that help individuals repent of the sin of homosexuality as a first step in transforming their lives.

In March 2003, the movement's website — www.transforming-cong.org — appeared to have been last updated in 2001. It said:

> Transforming Congregations affirm the biblical witness that:
> • Homosexual practice is sin: Leviticus 18:22; 20:13; Romans 1:26-27; 1 Corinthians 6:9-11; 1 Timothy 1:9-10.
> • The power of the Holy Spirit is available to transform the life of all persons, including the homosexual: 1 Corinthians 6:9-11; Romans 12:2; Galatians 5:16-25; 1 Peter 2:24.
>
> We seek to heal homosexual persons, their families and the Church. We minister to the needs of all persons affected by homosexuality, utilizing the resources from both within and

outside the Church in order to facilitate healing and whole-
ness: Romans 15:1-2; Galatians 6:1-2. We integrate all re-
pentant, redeemed persons, including homosexuals, into active membership and participation in the life of the Church.

In 1999, the movement listed 75 member churches, most United Methodist. About half were in California and Pennsylvania.

Coalition for United Methodist Accountability

In February 2000, representatives of Good News, the Confessing Movement, and the Institute on Religion and Democracy established yet another group — the Coalition for United Methodist Accountability.

The coalition's steering committee includes three representatives
from each of the founding groups. A Feb. 16, 2000, press release, states
the steering committee had assembled a team of attorneys and legal advisors to address the committee's concerns about accountability in the
order and administration of the church.

Citing "increasing disobedience to church doctrine and standards,
neglect of due process, and unfair administration on the part of some
bishops and district superintendents," coalition leaders have vowed to
seek remedies within the church. They will also seek remedies in constitutional law, they said.[44]

A Sept. 8, 2000, press release from the coalition said it had assisted
and will continue to assist "local clergy and laity in responding to other
clergy, district superintendents and bishops who are persistently ne-
glecting church law. Responses have included the filing of charges
against church leaders, where a conviction can mean a suspension or
removal from the ordained ministry."

Contact names on the press releases include:[45]

• Good News: James V. Heidinger II and Phil Granger;
• Confessing Movement: Patricia Miller and Ira Gallaway;
• Institute on Religion and Democracy: Thomas C. Oden; and
• Coalition legal coordinator: John Stumbo.

Endnotes

[1] Keysor "The Story…"; Robb 48; Neil 68.
[2] Keysor "Methodism's Silent…."
[3] Ibid.

[4] Robb 49; Heidinger "A History of Renewal."

[5] Heidinger "A History of Renewal."

[6] Keysor "The Story of Good News."

[7] Keysor "In the Aftermath..." 45.

[8] Ibid 38.

[9] Keysor "Confronting the Cults" 9.

[10] Keysor "The Gathering Storm" 19-23.

[11] The group now known as Affirmation: United Methodists for Lesbian, Gay, Bisexual, and Transgender Concerns was not formed until July 1975 See "A Brief History of Affirmation," http://www.umaffirm.org/afhistory.html> 15 March 2003.

[12] McClain 2.

[13] Two examples: 1. Keysor wrote, "In 1968, an unofficial group known as Methodists for Church Renewal *blitzkrieged* General Conference. In 1970, another unofficial group, the Black Methodists for Church Renewal seemed to dominate" (Keysor "Political Action" 27). 2. His description of New York Annual Conference's decision to retain the Rev. Paul Abels, an openly gay man, as pastor of Washington Square United Methodist Church was vivid: "It was a sad, familiar story of caucus *blitzkrieg:* a tightly disciplined group, actually a minority of the whole, exerting its will by means of superior discipline, commitment, and sacrifice. This is how the homosexual victory was won." (Keysor "Here We Go..." 62).

[14] For example, in 1974, Keysor wrote, "With growing indignation we have watched the United Methodist Council on Youth Ministries (UMCYM) become an outspoken advocate of ordaining practicing homosexuals.... What sort of church organization wishes to have sex perverts preaching to us....?" (Keysor "Leprosy..." 56, 57.) He called for the dismantling of UMCYM saying that it had betrayed "our church," the Gospel, and the "good-hearted trusting laypeople who gave their dollars...." He concluded, "May God use the righteous indignation of His People to remove this leprosy from the Body of Christ!" (Keysor "Leprosy..." 62.)

[15] Woodson 23-28.

[16] Robb 50.

[17] Good News 1997, 1998, 1999 IRS Form 990.

[18] Brown and Brown "'Good News' Movement Seeks Traditional...."

[19] http://www.renewnetwork.org as appeared 23 March 2003.

[20] http://www.renewnetwork.org as appeared 23 March 2003.

[21] Short, Renew letter February 2001.

[22] "Annual Book Review" *Good News* Sept/Oct 2002 31.

[23] "Mission Study Reviews" *Good News* Sept/Oct 2000 30.

[24] "Annual Book Review" *Good News* Sept/Oct 2002 30.

[25] Short "We Have a Vision" *Renew Newsletter* Winter 2001, Vol. 8, No. 4.

[26] *Renew Newsletter* Winter 2001, Vol. 8, No.4; *Good News* May/June 2002 31.

[27] *Good News* May/June 2002 30.

[28] Short Renew letter March 2002.

[29] Much of the information on The Mission Society for United Methodists comes from its website: http://wwwmsum.org as appeared 23 March 2003.

[30] Ewing Carroll telephone interview.

[31] "Report of Independent Public Accountant," MSUM December 31, 2001 and 2000.

[32] http://wwwconfessingumc.org as appeared on 23 March 2003.

[33] The Confessing Movement "Information" http://www.confessingumc.org/information. html as appeared 23 March 2003.

[34] "Be Steadfast" as appeared 23 March 203 at http://www.confessingumc.org/ conf_theolog_besteadfast.htm.

[35] *Good News* website 1 April 2003 http://www.goodnewsmag.org/renewal/junaluska.htm.

[36] *Good News* website 1 April 2003 http://www.goodnewsmag.org/renewal/junaluska.htm.

[37] *Good News* website 23 March 2003 <www.goodnewsmag.org>.

[38] *Good News* website 23 March 2003 <www.goodnewsmag.org>.

[39] Heidinger "Can We Recover...."

[40] Association for Church Renewal.

[41] Heidinger "A Brief History."

[42] http://catalystresources.org as appeared on 18 March 2003.

[43] IRS Form 990.

[44] Coalition for United Methodist Accountability "Renewal Groups Established...."

[45] Coalition for United Methodist Accountability "Coalition Planning...."

A Story
You've Got to Be Kidding

Look up "The Rev. Mary Kraus" using the Google Internet search engine. The first few listings confirm her position as a United Methodist pastor. They are followed by a lectionary commentary she wrote for her annual conference newspaper and the sermon she preached Sept. 16, 2001.

Then a few lines down, "Mary Kraus" is listed under "Occult." Click on this entry. An article pops up about "Wicca/Witchcraft Infiltrating Churches and Denominations."[1] Can this article be about the same Mary Kraus — pastor of Dumbarton United Methodist Church in Washington, D.C. for the past 13 years; a former missionary to Brazil; and a former district superintendent in Baltimore-Washington Conference? The article under the "Occult" heading implies that Mary Kraus is a dangerous "witch" who is "undermining the ministry" of other pastors through her teaching of false doctrine and participation in pagan rituals.[2]

Not only is this article about the same Mary Kraus who is a respected United Methodist pastor, it is a call by the Institute on Religion and Democracy (IRD) for her to lose her clergy credentials.

Kraus explained:

> At the end of December 1998, I was notified formal complaints had been filed against me. My immediate response to my bishop was that I was more than a little curious about what I had done to warrant such a dubious honor. I quickly

learned that I and colleague and friend, Nancy Webb, had been served with the following complaints:

• Engaging in practices declared by The United Methodist Church to be incompatible with Christian teaching,
• Disseminating doctrines contrary to the established standards of doctrine of the church, and
• Engaging in relationships and/or behavior that undermines the ministry of another pastor.

I was mystified about what I had managed to do that would cause a clergy colleague to file such an action. I did not know the Rev. Karen Booth before this time and was taken aback that a clergywoman would do this without any prior contact with me. I still did not know what I had done but then was told that it related to articles that Nancy and I had written about my 50th birthday celebration on New Year's Eve 1993.

We had been asked to write an article for the clergy-women's publication *WellSprings* on the ritual of croning that was designed to celebrate this transition. For those unfamiliar with the term, *croning* refers to a ceremony based on an ancient practice that celebrates a woman's passage into her older years. It honors the wisdom she has amassed over several decades and nurtures a positive self-image. This ceremony has experienced a renewal in recent years and is celebrated by women in all walks of life.

Nancy Webb and Rebecca Ruth Richards wrote about the fun they had designing my croning celebration. I explained why such a ritual was important to me, and the wonderful way it helped me embrace my 50 years of living. It had been empowering and life-giving.

It took some time for me to realize that this complaint was real, that Karen Booth and Elaine Wood, lay leader of a United Methodist church in Delaware, saw this private birthday party as a pagan ritual so dangerous I ought to be removed from pastoral ministry.

As Kraus proceeded through the complaint process, she was accused of such things as being steeped in pagan knowledge, advocating non-Christian beliefs and potentially leading young people astray. The experience became unnerving and demoralizing.

"It was like a force was trying to suck life out of me," Kraus said, adding she found herself on the defensive.

> No matter how ridiculous I knew this whole thing was, those bringing charges weren't about to listen to my perspective. No matter how hard I tried to engage them in a dialogue, the response would be a challenging re-statement of what they felt were the grievous actions I had committed. They shaped it as a power struggle to 'get' those whom they saw as having done something anti-Christian.
>
> I found myself moving in a world of distortion. Karen Booth held a premise that my birthday party was a pagan ritual. Because I had written about it in a published journal, I had caused serious damage to her ministry. Everything Karen said indicated that this had to be 'exorcized' from The United Methodist Church. That meant my credentials should be revoked.
>
> When the bishop offered the service of a mediator to work with us in further conversation, Nancy Webb and I agreed to meet if a mediator was present. Karen Booth and Elaine Wood declined to participate since they disagreed that any common ground could be found.

It was at this point that Booth and Wood published an account of the supervisory sessions. The bishop had explained that the sessions he conducted were to be confidential. The charges against Kraus never went beyond this first level of inquiry because confidentiality had been broken.

"The article by Booth and Wood is filled with distortions and unfounded accusations," Kraus said. It first appeared on the Unofficial Confessing Movement's website — www.ucmpage.org — under UM Accountability Watch.[3] The next month, Mark Tooley ran an article in *UMAction,* an IRD publication.[4]

The article was brought to Kraus' attention by members of her church who enjoyed ribbing her about the charges of witchcraft.

"We just couldn't believe it," church member Ginny Lapham said.

"Mary is a remarkable pastor and a woman of deep Christian faith."

So how is it Kraus' name appears under the "Occult" in the Google search? The occult website picked up the Unofficial Confessing Movement website article from the IRD website.[5]

Endnotes

[1] "The Occult."
[2] UCMPage.org "United Methodist…."
[3] UCMPage.org "Published "Croning."
[4] Tooley "A Crone Bishop."
[5] "The Occult."

2
The Institute on Religion and Democracy

The stories exploded like hand grenades in the ecumenical world.

They began in *Reader's Digest*. In August 1982, it blasted the World Council of Churches with an article that asked, "Karl Marx or Jesus Christ?" In January 1983, *Reader's Digest* had another question: "Do you know where your church dollars go?" The ominous subtitle: "You better find out because they may be supporting revolutions rather than religion."

Also in January 1983, CBS's "60 Minutes" carried harsh and distorted attacks on the World and National Councils of Churches, especially their ties to Third-World liberation groups such as the anti-apartheid South African Council of Churches. False accusations of giving funds to armed insurgents were framed as questions, an apparent attempt to avoid slander charges.

Twenty years later, Don Hewitt, creator and still producer of the program, was asked on the Dec. 2, 2002, "Larry King Live" show if he regretted any show in "60 Minutes" 36-year history. "Yes," he answered. "We once took off on the National Council of Churches (NCC) as being left-wing and radical and a lot of nonsense."

The morning after the NCC "60 Minutes," he got congratulatory calls from several right-wing sources. He thought: "We must have done something wrong last night, and I think we probably did."

Four articles appeared in *The New York Times* within 15 months with headlines like: "New Church Group Assails Aid to Leftists."[1]

All these stories had been initiated by the Institute on Religion and Democracy (IRD). It had hit the ground running after its 1981 founding. It and some of its founders were featured in each of the stories. Who are those guys, asked stunned ecumenical participants from around the world? And what motivates them?

Those questions remain more than 20 years later. That's true for thousands of people who unexpectedly receive mailings from IRD each year. Some question the allegations. Others accept the innuendo as fact.

Original IRD leaders included two men nationally known as former anti-Vietnam war figures who had moved right after the 1960s with a small band of East-Coast intellectuals known as *neoconservatives.* Richard John Neuhaus, now a Roman Catholic priest, and Michael Novak, prominent Catholic layman, then and now are key IRD figures. Neuhaus, who heads the Institute for Religion and Public Life in New York City, drafted IRD's founding document, available on IRD's website — www.ird-renew.org. Novak left an academic career in the 1970s to bring religious inquiry to the corporate think tank, the American Enterprise Institute.

Neuhaus and Novak were joined by two more neoconservatives who had moved from left to right on the political spectrum — Penn Kemble and David Jessup. Kemble, associate director of the U.S. Information Agency in the Clinton Administration, was at that time a political organizer. Jessup worked for the AFL-CIO.

In the first IRD public activity, Jessup, one month after joining a United Methodist church, attended the 1980 United Methodist General Conference where he presented what came to be known as the "Jessup Report," a critical analysis of church activity, to a side meeting.[2]

George Weigel, now senior fellow at the Ethics and Public Policy Center and known for an extensive biography of Pope Paul II, associated with IRD in 1984 before he moved to Washington, D.C., from the World Without War Council in Seattle, Washington.

Neuhaus, Novak, Kemble, Jessup and Weigel added United Methodist Evangelist Edmund W. Robb Jr. from Texas, a mainstay of Good News, to the mix. He shared little experience with the other five. Robb became IRD president and its public face. Early on, he appeared in a public-television documentary with Ben Wattenberg — still on television in "Think Tank with Ben Wattenberg" — attacking church leaders called "Protestants Protest." Robb was the sole protestor. Penn Kemble produced the show.[3]

Robb's IRD involvement — along with that of another United Methodist, Ira Gallaway, long-time Good News activist and currently assistant executive director of the Confessing Movement — meant United Methodists would be first in the line of fire.

IRD was created and sustained with money from right-wing corporate foundations described in Chapter 8. Such foundations supplied more than 80 percent of IRD's income during its first decade. From 1981-2001, IRD received about $4.4 million from these nonreligious entities.[4]

Novak; Neuhaus; Robb; Weigel; Gallaway; and Robb's son, Ed Robb III — pastor of a large United Methodist church in The Woodlands, Texas, and executive director of A Foundation for Theological Education, which funds theological doctoral work for orthodox students — remain on IRD's Board of Directors. Their long-time leadership means IRD's core vision remains. The board has continuity and strong connections with other conservative renewal groups.

The staff also displays continuity. IRD President Diane Knippers left her post as an editor at *Good News* magazine to join IRD's staff in 1982. Knippers became the institute's president in 1993. She oversees the Episcopal effort. Mark Tooley — a CIA employee for eight years — has been at IRD since 1994. He directs UMAction, the IRD subsidiary focusing on The United Methodist Church. Alan Wisdom, who has been on the IRD staff since 1983, heads the Presbyterian committee. Together, Knippers, Tooley and Wisdom have more than 50 years working in the conservative renewal movement.

IRD: The Institution

When IRD hit the jackpot with its media coverage in 1982, it barely had staff and shared an office. Its current nine-person staff is located in the center of think-tank Washington, D.C. Its 2001 revenues were $1,120,508 compared to $777,654 in 2000 and $818,380 in 1999.[5] Knippers said individual contributions have reduced foundation dependence to about 30 percent.[6]

Other members of IRD's self-selecting board include:
• Mary Ellen Bork, wife of controversial judge, Robert Bork;

- Journalist Fred Barnes, executive editor and a founder of *The Weekly Standard,* a conservative news magazine; co-host of Fox-TV's "Beltway Boys; and regular on Fox-TV's "Special Report";
- Terry Schlossberg, chair of Presbyterians Pro-Life; and
- Robert George, conservative Princeton University legal theorist, also on the board of the Ethics and Public Policy Center and the editorial panel for *First Things,* Neuhaus' journal. He directs the James Madison Program at Princeton, which in 2001 got $380,000 from John M. Olin Foundation and Lynde and Harry Bradley Foundation, two of the foundations that sustain IRD.[7]
- John Boone, secretary of the IRD board, is a director of the Presbyterian Lay Committee.

Also on the IRD board are wealthy individuals:

- Roberta Green Ahmanson, wife of Howard Fieldstead Ahmanson, heir to the California-based Home Savings and Loan fortune, who recently began to finance the American Anglican Council. Among Howard Ahmanson's many political engagements was a $350,000 donation to back Proposition 209 in California, which bans affirmative action in state institutions and contracting.[8]
- David Stanley, chair of UM Action, a board member of the United Methodist Confessing Movement, founder and CEO of Pearl Mutual Funds, and chair of the National Taxpayers Union.
- United Methodist Helen Rhea Stumbo, first vice chair of IRD and a former president of the Good News board, an heiress of the Blue Bird bus fortune.

Thomas C. Oden, professor of theology and ethics at Drew Theological School, is chair of the IRD board. He convened the confessing theologians group that prepared a statement for the October 2002 Association for Church Renewal meeting in Indianapolis. Oden published a book of essays in 2002 called *A Return to Orthodoxy.*

In reviewing Oden's book, Jeffrey Gros of the U.S. Conference of Catholic Bishops, said it is permeated by "disillusionment, anger and even sarcasm." Gros says the book contributes to appreciation of the Christian heritage but when Oden addresses individuals and institutions with which he disagrees, the book "falls far short of the facts and of the Christian fairness that is the scholar's calling."[9]

IRD's Agenda

What are IRD's priorities today? IRD laid out its priorities in 2000 in a funding proposal called "Reforming America's Churches Project: 2001-2004." (The Executive Summary is in the Appendix.) The proposal says the institute's program "for influencing the governing church conventions of three denominations will cost over $3.6 million over the next four years."

How much of that amount would be in addition to IRD's core budget is not clear. IRD's income increase of $350,000 from 2000 to 2001 fell well short of the goal. *UMAction,* while asking for donations in January 2003, reported 2002 had not been a good year financially.

More than half of the $3.6 million was projected for the United Methodist effort. The funding proposal says:

> IRD is giving special attention to reform of The United Methodist Church, America's third largest religious body and the largest denomination under religious left control.[10]

IRD summarized its work:

> IRD was founded in 1981 to combat the irresponsible political lobbying of mainline churches. Much of IRD's initial focus was upon directly countering the influence of church leaders in religious and secular elites. Our more recent emphasis is upon directly reaching millions of American churchgoers through the media, coalition building and our own publications.

IRD organizes around the following issues:
- Marriage and sexuality: It opposes feminist activity, gay rights and abortion;
- Environmentalism: It opposes environmental initiatives, specifically the Kyoto Accords;
- Hate crimes: It opposes hate-crimes legislation;
- Federal social entitlements: It opposes government responsibility to provide a safety net for the poor;
- National security: It supports the war on terrorism and the war in Iraq, and opposes those who don't.

IRD works in coalitions, including with the Association for Church Renewal. IRD helped create this joint work by conservative renewal groups from major mainline churches. (See Chapter 1.)

"The Association for Church Renewal allows us to synchronize strategies across denominational lines," the funding proposal says.

IRD President Knippers is active in the schismatic American Anglican Council. Founded in Texas six years ago but now based in Washington, D.C., the council focuses on homosexuality. It aligns itself with bishops from other countries to give legitimacy to dissident priests in the United States.[11]

The funding proposal states:

> We will annually prepare resolutions for local and regional church conventions in the three major denominations (United Methodist, Presbyterian and Episcopal)....Working with other renewal organizations, we will identify electable conservative candidates for national church committees....

Using the Media

IRD's primary tactic remains to magnify its mission "to discredit and diminish the Religious Left's influence" through the media. It says it has a list of 1,000 media contacts to which it sends material regularly, including "every major religion writer in the country (and) every major religious magazine."

Knippers is regularly quoted in religion stories that share perspectives from left to right ends of the spectrum. She serves on the board of *Christianity Today,* an evangelical journal. Alan Wisdom writes for *Presbyterian Layman,* the Presbyterian equivalent to *Good News* magazine. Mark Tooley is on the Good News board and often writes for *Good News* magazine.

A search of *The New York Times* archives since 1996 does not suggest a repeat of IRD's early success there. Its most common secular outlets appear to be through *The Washington Times, Insight* magazine and United Press International — all owned by Sun Myung Moon's Unification Church.

IRD mounts its most direct attacks in its own publications. Its quarterly, *Faith and Freedom,* was sent to 12,000 donors and others in 2000. *Episcopal Action* and *Presbyterian Action* went to a total of 8,000 people. IRD predicted a near doubling of those numbers by 2004.

The IRD funding proposal said *UMAction's* distribution was 275,000 in 2000 with a goal of 500,000 by 2004. Mark Tooley said in a phone interview in March 2003 that distribution was about 315,000, the same as a year earlier.

It's hard to measure the effectiveness of publications that are sent free to households across the United States. It's far different from tracking paid subscribers. Numerous recipients report receiving multiple copies unsolicited. One person, who serves on a number of church entities, said a few years ago he received 20 copies of the *Presbyterian Layman,* sent, its editors say, to 600,000 readers.

Three organizations that have been targeted by *UMAction* in recent months were asked what happened. The United Methodist General Board of Church and Society said no article had ever generated more than 12 critical letters, phone calls and e-mails. The Women's Division of the United Methodist General Board of Global Ministries said it once received 26 such communications. The Methodist Federation for Social Action received five.

Nonetheless, IRD's attacks do extract a bitter toll. Read the stories in this book of people and churches who became targets of opportunity for IRD.

When Tooley was asked how he responds to the criticism that his work is too polemical, he said: "Polemics have their place. My purpose is to write in a style that will appeal to and clarify for our readers."

IRD's barrage of accusations and distortions requires critical reading and analysis. An illustration of how to do that is in Chapter 3. Another follows.

Ron Sider Exposes UM Action

Evangelical professor and social-justice advocate Ron Sider and his colleague Jim Ball responded to an article that involved them. Tooley attacked an undefined "Religious Left" for joining a campaign against sports utility vehicles (SUVs) and other road hogs that consume large quantities of gas and pollute extensively:[12]

> The Religious Left has joined the secular left in its campaign against SUVs and other monster vehicles that Americans enjoy driving.

Tooley picked on the wrong people. Sider and Ball riddled his article. Excerpts follow. Tooley's article and the Sider-Ball response are available in full on IRD's website.[13]

Sider and Ball said:

> Mr. Tooley states that "What Would Jesus Drive?" (WWJD) is a question being put forward by "liberal ecclesiastics" and is being waged by the National Council of Churches, the Coalition on the Environment and Jewish Life, and our organization, the Evangelical Environmental Network. This is simply incorrect...WWJDrive is a campaign led by evangelical Christians. Prominent evangelical Christian leaders have publicly endorsed our campaign....
>
> As evangelical leaders, we are raising the question "What Would Jesus Drive?" because we consider our transportation choices to be moral questions. Why? Today's transportation choices are related to three serious problems: (1) pollution's impact on human health, especially children's health, (2) the threat of global warming, and (3) our dependence on foreign oil from unstable regions. Mr. Tooley reported primarily only one of these concerns, global warming....
>
> Mr. Tooley wrote that our position understood relations with Iraq to be "just" about oil. To say that one aspect of U.S. relations with Iraq is about oil is in no way to say that our relations with Iraq are only about oil. That statement by Mr. Tooley is false. Absolutely nothing in our analysis or statements suggests anything of the sort....
>
> We also find it astonishing that Mr. Tooley would say that WWJDrive's policy work is somehow inappropriate because it "diverts the Christian church away from its primary task — proclaiming the gospel."
>
> The IRD does political work all the time. Is that diverting the Church from its primary task of evangelism? Surely one of the great advances in evangelical thinking in the last few decades is to understand that biblical Christians must combine evangelism and social action. It is puzzling to see Mr. Tooley repeating an old one-sided notion that virtually all evangelical leaders have rejected.

Stumbling on the War

IRD tried to stir up emotion against objections to the Iraq war in the churches it monitors. Michael Novak was invited by the U.S. ambassador to the Vatican to come to Rome to defend the U.S. position. He, John Neuhaus and George Weigel — the neoconservative IRD core — were identified as "Catholic Hawks" in a March 2003 Religion News Service article.[14]

Diane Knippers wrote that the anti-war church leaders did not have sufficient intelligence data and expertise to make such judgments. She wrote of the decision to go to war: "It is a lay vocation — the responsibility of people with the expertise and the information."[15] Does she not know of the Bay of Pigs fiasco or remember Vietnam?

IRD had to attack those opposed to the war gingerly because the National Association of Evangelicals, for which Knippers is an officer, declined to pass a resolution backing the U.S. government's Iraq policy. In spite of support for the war from white evangelical laity in the United States, evangelical leaders worried about the 600,000 Christians in Iraq, the future and safety of mission work, and the danger of turning the conflict into a Muslim-Christian conflict. A few rejected it on just-war grounds.[16]

IRD hit the National Council of Churches for criticizing Jerry Falwell when he called the Prophet Muhammad a "terrorist." Tooley wrote:

> When Falwell used the word "terrorist," under his questioner's prompting, he was probably guilty of rhetorical overreach. In the same way, religious left-wingers have come to call world hunger, disease and global debt examples of "terrorism."[17]

Notice no one is identified as using terrorism in this way. It also seems strange he would bring up those powerful concerns since they are so absent from IRD's agenda.

National Association of Evangelicals Vice President Richard Cizik said in a telephone interview, "Evangelicals shuddered when some high profile people disparaged Islam."

Perhaps Tooley's most widely picked-up article came out just after President George W. Bush's inauguration. It discussed what it meant to have a Methodist as president. His crystal ball was cloudy on one point at least. He wrote:

> Methodists abhor debt. It is suitable that Bush may be al-
> most the first president since Andrew Jackson to pay off the
> national debt.[18]

Two years later, the budget surplus Bush inherited is gone. According to a Congressional Budget Office report in March 2003, the projected $5.6 trillion budget surplus for 2013 is now likely to be a $1.6 trillion deficit.[19]

IRD Continues

IRD, which supplies media troops for Good News and the United Methodist Confessing Movement, and their counterparts in other denominations, has never built its own constituency. While it challenges the accountability of church agencies and staff, it remains a self-perpetuating institution accountable to no constituency that will challenge its words when they distort and distract. As someone said: "IRD's half-facts are like half-bricks. You can't build with them but you can throw them a long way."[20]

Peter Steinfels, now a religion writer at *The New York Times,* wrote in 1982 that IRD appeared to be "a conservative-neoconservative alliance intended to advance a distinct political agenda while claiming only a broad Christian concern."[21]

The years have confirmed his suspicion.

Endnotes

[1] Howell "Old Wine..." 50.
[2] Ibid.
[3] Ibid.
[4] The $44 million figure was arrived at like this: The Media Transparency Project documented grants from conservative secular foundations of $3,579,000 between 1985 and 2001. Source: www.mediatransparency.org. About $479,500 arrived from December 1980 through January 1983 from the same foundations. Source: *Christianity and Crisis,* 23 March 1983. Total: $4,058,500. That leaves 1983-1984 to be accounted for. (Assume an annual average of $200,000.) That totals $4,458,000 from 1981 through 2001.
[5] IRD IRS 990: 2001.
[6] Siemon-Netto.
[7] Grant Data Project.
[8] CPER Alert.
[9] Gros 32.
[10] Much of the data in this section comes from the funding request. See the "Executive Summary" in the Appendix.

[11] Knippers "Legislative...."
[12] Tooley "What Would...."
[13] Sider and Ball.
[14] White.
[15] Knippers "Being Anti...."
[16] Broadway B9.
[17] "Church Officials...."
[18] Tooley "A Methodist Moment in Washington."
[19] Congressional Budget Office "An Analysis of the President's Budgetary Proposals for Fiscal Year 2004."
[20] Scott.
[21] Steinfels.

3
The UM Action Method

A copy of the May 2002 *UMAction* newsletter showed up in the Tidewater, Virginia, mailbox of Clyde Decker, a retired naval architect and a lifelong United Methodist. He sent it to a friend with a handwritten note:

> Where does this stuff come from? I never asked for it. It's so
> nasty. The difference between the writer and me is that I love
> my church, warts and all. He seems to want to destroy it.

The cover of *UMAction* says 315,000 copies were mailed. Many recipients never asked for it. One way UM Action expands its mailing list is encouraging individuals to send in their local-church directories.

The May 2002 issue invites an in-depth look at how its publisher, the Institute on Religion and Democracy (IRD), attempts to manipulate readers on an emotional subject.

How to respond to threats of violence is worthy of debate. In the winter of 2003 before the Iraq war began, the moral pros and cons were examined in many places, church settings prominent among them. Especially within the life of the church, such debate deserves to be conducted with care, respect and fairness.

That did not happen here. It occurs too rarely in IRD material.

Here are three examples of how statements by official United Methodist bodies were summarized in *UMAction* in ways that distort. Note how different reality is when compared to the IRD charges. The full statements are in the Appendix. *UMAction* Editor Mark Tooley opened with a greeting and question:

> Dear United Methodist Friend, Did you know that United Methodist leaders are undermining the U.S. war against terrorism?

He followed with questions.

Tooley: Did you know that our denomination's Board of Church and Society has voted to oppose the U.S. war against terror?"

Here's a small part of what the United Methodist General Board of Church and Society actually said Oct. 13, 2001:

> We claim the teachings of the Prince of Peace who instructs us to love and pray for our enemies and refrain from responding to violence with violence. As we join people around the world in our resolve to bring terrorists to justice, we understand that war is not an appropriate means of responding to criminal acts against humanity.

> We reaffirm The United Methodist resolution on "Terrorism" (No. 317 in *The Book of Resolutions of The United Methodist Church, 2000)* that states, "We oppose the use of indiscriminate military force to combat terrorism, especially where the use of such force results in casualties among non-combatant citizens who are not themselves perpetrators of terrorist acts..." We condemn all acts of terrorism, with no exception for the target or the source.[1]

Tooley: Did you know that the United Methodist Women's Division voted to oppose the U.S. bombing in Afghanistan?

Here's a part of what the Women's Division of the United Methodist General Board of Global Ministries approved in October 2001:

> As followers of Jesus Christ, we are called to choose life over death (Deuteronomy 30:19). We are also called to love our enemies and pray for those who persecute us (Matthew 5:44). As United Methodist Women, we are challenged to commit ourselves, through prayer, study and action, and to continue the search for peace with justice.

> We therefore call on United Methodist Women to urge the President to use diplomatic means to bring the perpetra-

tors of terrorists acts to justice and to end the bombing of Afghanistan. Countries of the South as well as the North must be involved as decision makers in addressing efforts to combat terrorism.[2]

Tooley: Did you know that the United Methodist Council of Bishops renounced all violence, refusing to differentiate between acts of terror and the U.S. military response?

Here's a small part of what the United Methodist Council of Bishops said Nov. 9, 2001:

> We, your bishops, believe that violence in all of its forms and expressions is contrary to God's purpose for the world. Violence creates fear, desperation, hopelessness and instability. We call upon the church to be a community of peace with justice and to support individuals and agencies all over the world who are working for the common good for all of God's children. We also call upon the church to study and work toward alleviating the root causes of poverty and the other social conditions that are exploited by terrorists.[3]

Tooley concluded:

> I believe these actions are scandalous. They do not represent the views of the vast majority of United Methodists. I bet they don't represent your views. They certainly don't represent mine.
>
> More importantly, I believe official United Methodist opposition to the war against terror contradicts the testimony of Scripture and the thinking of most Christians for 2,000 years. St. Paul wrote that the state has a responsibility to "wield the sword" in defense of its citizens.

Taking a Close Look

▶ **Tooley: "Official United Methodist opposition to the war against terror"?** Nowhere in the agencies' statements is Tooley's claim demonstrable.

▶ **Tooley: "Contradicts the testimony of Scripture"?** Tooley is proof-texting. All can play that game.

▶ **Tooley: "Wield the sword"?** What of Jesus' admonition that "all who take up the sword will perish by the sword" (Matthew 26:52)? What of those earlier words of Isaiah, repeated by Micah, compelling all nations "to beat their swords into plowshares" and "to learn war no more" (Isaiah 2:4, Micah 4:3)?

And what was Paul saying at the beginning of Romans 13, the passage Tooley quotes? Check Romans 12:19-20:

> Beloved, never avenge yourselves, but leave it to the wrath of God; for it is written, "Vengeance is mine. I will repay says the Lord. No, if your enemy is hungry, feed him; if he is thirsty, give him drink...."

Most scholars conclude that the Greek word translated *sword* in Romans 13:4 identifies the symbol of authority carried by the police who accompanied tax collectors. Paul was not arguing for war but rather for peace — Christians pay your taxes, do not rebel, as rumor suggested you might. Tooley distorts the text.[4]

▶ **Tooley: Agencies' statements contradict "the thinking of most Christians for 2,000 years"?** Certainly not that of the early Christian communities, who refused all forms of military service. Certainly not the thinking of Methodism founder John Wesley.

In a recent feature for United Methodist News Service titled "At the Roots of Methodism: Wesley Abhorred 'Curse' of War," British Methodist journalist John Singleton wrote of Wesley: "He could not be described as a pacifist....nevertheless he believed war to be the 'foulest curse' on the face of humanity."[5]

Wesley, in his 1757 Doctrine of Original Sin, wrote:

> There is a still more horrid reproach to the Christian name, yea, to the name of man, to all reason and humanity. There is war in the world! War between men! War between Christians! I mean between those that bear the name of *Christ* [italics in original], and profess to *walk as he taught us to walk* [italics in original]. Now who can reconcile War, I will not say to Religion, but to any degree of reason or common sense?...What an amazing way of deciding controversies.[6]

Endnotes

[1] General Board of Church and Society "Statement to the Church...."

[2] General Board of Global Ministries, Women's Division, "Resolution on Terrorist Attacks" October 2001 board meeting.

[3] Council of Bishops of The United Methodist Church Pastoral Letter.

[4] Stassen Ch 9.

[5] Singleton "At the Roots of Methodism...."

[6] Wesley IX: 56-57.

A Story

An IRD Target

Debate is no stranger to J. Philip Wogaman, who spent 26 years teaching Christian ethics — 11 as dean — at Wesley Theological Seminary in Washington, D.C. Still, Wogaman, whose books are used in theological seminaries across the country, never expected charges that he espouses art portraying Jesus as a drag queen.

But that's what happened in 1992 when he became pastor of historic 1,400-member Foundry United Methodist Church in Washington, D.C. His notoriety did not come from stands he took on knotty moral questions — he has never been afraid to do that — but arose because former President Bill Clinton and First Lady Hillary Clinton chose to worship at Foundry.

That put a bull's-eye on Wogaman. The Institute on Religion and Democracy (IRD) labeled Foundry the "Clintons' church" and Wogaman the "president's pastor."

Mark Tooley, *UMAction* editor and coordinator for IRD's United Methodist campaign, showed up at Sunday services.

Following are examples of how IRD singled out Wogaman:

▶ **The Drag-Queen Incident**
Tooley attended a Saturday event at Foundry United Methodist Church sponsored by Parents, Families, Friends of Lesbians and Gays (PFLAG), then wrote a press release. He reported Wogaman's response

when asked about the possibility of showing Christ as a drag queen. Tooley quoted Wogaman as saying, "I don't condemn it. I just don't know. I'll have to think about it."[1]

The drag queen phrase got picked up by media around the country. One version appeared several places with the headline, "Was Jesus a Drag Queen?" Another report characterized Wogaman's statement as "a blasphemous message delivered from the pulpit." A third judged that "the homosexual bash at Clinton's church proved that today's society is even more debauched and perverse (than Sodom and Gomorrah). Mark Tooley, a Methodist layman who attended, provided us this shocking report...."[2]

This is what happened. Wogaman agreed to do a workshop on homosexuality and religion. About 100 people filled a chapel at the church. At the end of his talk, he answered questions participants had written on index cards. One question referred to H. Richard Niebuhr's classic book, *Christ and Culture*. It said:

> We're familiar with stained-glass windows depicting an African Christ figure. What would it mean to depict Christ as a drag queen?

Wogaman's reply, taken from a tape of the event, was:

> Well. (Pause.) That's an interesting question. (Audience laughter.) I suspect the drag phenomenon is probably pathological. It's a response. I don't condemn it, but I think it is a response born out of persecution, abuse, at least as I understand it, an in-your-face kind of thing. On the other hand, I'll have to think about it some more.

▶ Distortion of Ministry

Tooley wrote a profile of Wogaman called "The President's Pastor" that appeared in IRD's spring 1995 issue of its *Faith and Freedom* quarterly. It mixed pleasant comments — "Tall, slender and adorned in a white robe, he presides over the service elegantly, with a professorial voice and wry humor" — with digs — "Liberal yuppies may find inspiration in Wogaman's urbane, modern theology...but working-class people with traditionalist views may prefer the 'crutch' of biblical literalism against which Wogaman has preached."[3]

Wogaman said of Tooley's profile: "It's distorted my whole ministry by quoting things out of context and focusing on a few points."

Tooley's article got to syndicated columnist Cal Thomas, a former spokesperson for Jerry Falwell's Moral Majority. Thomas, without talking to Wogaman, wrote a column on Wogaman that ran in papers across the country.[4]

In the summer 1995 issue of *Faith and Freedom,* IRD took credit for Thomas' column.

Wogaman retired as pastor of Foundry in 2002. He had written a book, *From The Eye of the Storm,* about his role as one of President Clinton's spiritual counselors when the president faced impeachment in 1998. Wogaman is teaching a class at Wesley Theological Seminary; is writing a book; and writes a regular column for *Zion's Herald,* a bi-monthly magazine published by the Boston Wesleyan Association.

In the March-April 2003 *Zion's Herald,* Wogaman says he is disturbed by what he calls "hard ball in the church of Jesus Christ." He wrote:

> Disagreements, faced honestly, can lead us all to better practices and clearer understandings of theological truth....What is to be said, now, to the strident voices tempting us to use raw power to resolve conflicts of mind and spirit? Surely the answer is that we cannot let harsh rhetoric and hard tactics undermine mutual confidence and mutual respect in the life of the church. We should be more gentle in the church of Jesus Christ. We are on holy ground.[5]

Endnotes

[1] Tooley "Homosexuals, the Episcopal Bishop, and the President's Pastor."
[2] Marrs.
[3] Tooley "The President's Pastor."
[4] Thomas "Politics and the Pastor."
[5] Wogaman "Playing Hardball on Holy Ground."

4
Attacks from the Right

- United Methodist Women/Women's Division of the United Methodist General Board of Global Ministries,
- General Board of Church and Society,
- General Commission on the Status and Role of Women, and
- General Commission on Religion and Race.

These agencies of The United Methodist Church have something in common. They are all under attack with Good News and the Institute on Religion and Democracy calling for their elimination or drastic change.

United Methodist Women and Women's Division Under Fire

One significant faith-sustaining inspiration over the years and today is the untiring, imaginative energy women give to mission in our churches.

These women — brought together, trained and stimulated by United Methodist Women and its parent organization, the Women's Division of the United Methodist General Board of Global Ministries — are the ones most likely to share with us news from the world church. They read and discuss study books that expand their grasp of mission. They attend schools of Christian mission. They help move their churches into work with their neighbors, especially those in need.

They are prophetic. They reach out to the least of these — the women, children and youth of our nation and world, especially those without resources or voice. Close to 1 million members give more than $20 million a year for mission.

Opposition forces want to stand this dynamic on its head. Good News and its Renew Women's Network launched an attack on the Women's Division shortly after the 2000 General Conference. Misleadingly named "A Call for Reform of the Women's Division," Good News/Renew have put forth a plan that would dismantle the heart of women's ministry and leadership within the denomination.

Should this proposal succeed, women's historic leadership of mission work within the church would be undermined. The ability of women to decide how the money they raise for mission is spent would be usurped. Mission would be much more narrowly defined only as offering personal salvation, thus abandoning advocacy efforts toward a more just society for all God's children. Themes in the Good News/Renew plan are familiar:

• Lift up Christ and make sharing the Gospel our mission focus,
• Reform and reorganize the Women's Division,
• End unbiblical advocacy, and
• Promote real choice in women's programs.

▶ Lift up Christ and make sharing the Gospel our mission focus.

United Methodist Women's Purpose Statement reflects the reality that the organization is primarily focused on lifting up Christ and sharing the Gospel. The Purpose statement begins:

> The organized unit of United Methodist Women shall be a community of women whose Purpose is to know God and to experience freedom as whole persons through Jesus Christ....

Are United Methodist Women/Women's Division failing to lift up Christ and to share the Gospel? That depends on what it means to lift up Christ and to share the Gospel.

Renew is critical of Women's Division support of interfaith dialogue that seeks to bring understanding between faith groups. Renew would end such dialogue, shifting focus only to converting people to Christ.

The Good News/Renew plan calls for the Women's Division to "embrace the understanding that the Great Commission is given to men and women who are to work alongside each other for its fulfillment."

While this direction is not fully fleshed out, a look at how Good News and Renew relate is instructive.

Men dominate the Good News board — just seven of close to 40 directors are women. By contrast, the Women's Division directors are all women elected by women of the church. *Good News* magazine devotes one and occasionally two pages per issue to Renew women's news. The Women's Division publishes its own magazine — *Response* — 11 times a year with the magazine's full 48 pages devoted to interpretation of the women's mission program.

The result of the demand for "reform" would be to limit women's access to decision-making arenas. This has happened within denominations that have tried this. Among mainline Protestant denominations, only within The United Methodist Church — where the women's mission movement has retained its voice and worked for policies that maintain that voice — does a strong women's movement remain. Women from other denominations seek to emulate it. They recognize what they lost in the 1960s and 1970s when they merged their work with that of their denominations with no requirements for continuation of laywomen's leadership and decision-making.

▶ **Reform and reorganize the Women's Division.**

The Good News/Renew plan says:

> The Call for Reform seeks to end the Women's Division autonomy and formulate a structure with direct accountability to the whole church, including the General Council on Finance and Administration.

This statement falsely says the Women's Division is not fully accountable to the church. The Women's Division is not the free-standing, free-wheeling organization Good News/Renew would have people believe. The division is a unit of the United Methodist General Board of Global Ministries. It exists at the will of the General Conference. It is accountable to a board elected through United Methodist Women.

Proponents of the plan — themselves autonomous — are aware of the division's relationship to the whole church. That's why they have sought to use the General Conference's power over the division in resolutions to disband or weaken the organization.

A key example: Good News/Renew-supported legislation introduced at the 1996 and 2000 General Conferences that would have changed *Discipline* language that says local United Methodist Churches *shall* have a unit of United Methodist Women to *may* have a unit. This would reduce United Methodist Women to an optional women's organization within the denomination. A similar proposal to make United Methodist Women optional in local churches will appear in 2004 legislation.

The call to reorganize the division has three more points:
- Assure that evangelicals comprise at least 50 percent of the staff and elected directors of the Women's Division,
- Align Women's Division spending patterns with revised Women's Division/United Methodist Women standards, and
- Assure that the division adheres to open-meeting policy.

Key in this list is the call for changes in the spending patterns of United Methodist Women/Women's Division. Currently, they are allowed by the *Discipline* to raise and spend their own money.

When coupled with proposed governance changes, United Methodist Women/Women's Division would become a place for women to add to the coffers of the denomination without a leading say in how the money is spent.

► End unbiblical advocacy.

Progressive social-justice advocacy based on biblical mandates has been a hallmark of the women's mission movement since its inception. Women have led the church in key areas: racial justice, human rights, gender justice, an end to colonialism, peacemaking and more. This portion of the Good News/Renew plan would gut that gift to the church and community.

While wording of this theme appears to call the women into "accountability" to denominational positions, it is in fact a sweeping plan to remove women's ability to initiate social-justice efforts. Such work has always alarmed conservative factions within the denomination. The Good News/Renew effort to dismantle United Methodist Women/

Women's Division's successful work for justice is just the latest attempt to silence progressive women within the denomination.

This theme judges the women's work to be "unbiblical." Nothing could be further from the truth. The work of United Methodist Women/Women's Division is grounded in the ongoing revelation of Scripture. Members engage yearly in in-depth spiritual-growth studies, use monthly Bible studies from *Response* magazine, and set mission goals and directions guided by Scriptural teachings.

▶ Promote real choice in women's programs.

Good News/Renew sources explain this fourth theme as follows:

> The Call for Reform seeks to offer local choice for an alternative women's ministry or United Methodist Women or both....

Such a concept was defeated at General Conferences in 1996 and 2000. It will likely be a key issue at the 2004 General Conference. What's behind this move? Money. As part of this theme, Good News/Renew ask the denomination to "discontinue undesignated Pledge to Mission and put designated giving in its place."

Members of local units could override funding decisions made by the elected board of the Women's Division, the concern being that ongoing, long-supported projects could go begging as individual units responded to the best mailings from richer mission projects and personnel. Undesignated giving — giving to the budget of the Women's Division as established by division directors — has long provided assurance that support will continue to mission projects — some more than 100 years old. It also ensures supported projects and personnel meet criteria established by the women.

In Sum: Be Alert

Passing the Good News/Renew proposals for women's mission within the denomination would have two clear results:

• Women would be removed from their historic leadership in the denomination's mission program, and

• Women's voices would be silenced within the denomination's decision-making arenas.

"A Call for Reform" is in keeping with conservative Christian thinking that requires women to be subservient to men. Observe developments within the Southern Baptist Convention. The Baptist Faith and Message statement approved in 2000 limits ordination to men and says "a wife is to submit herself graciously to the servant leadership of her husband."

The Good News/Renew proposal is not about specific justice issues but about total structural overhaul that will push women out. Specific social-justice concerns — reproductive rights and other human rights of women — are at stake.

Be alert. While passionate debates on specific issues capture General Conference's attention, dry but crucial structural resolutions may pass without fanfare that would move women far from the decision-making table.

While short-term victories can be won on resolutions here and there, the long-term struggle will be lost if women are silenced.

Institute on Religion and Democracy Tries to Shut Down General Board of Church and Society

The United Methodist Building — 80 years old in 2004 — is an impressive presence in Washington, D.C. The U.S. Capitol rises to its immediate west. The U.S. Supreme Court sits just across the street to its south.

Methodists established the first permanent religious office in the nation's capital. Prohibition was the big concern then. In the decades since, United Methodists have witnessed, often prophetically, on a multitude of issues.

The building now houses the United Methodist General Board of Church and Society among other denominational and non-profit offices.

History has been made in the building. Martin Luther King Jr. had a space there as he helped to plan the 1963 March on Washington, site of his "I Have a Dream" speech. The first President Bush detailed a person from the White House to staff a coalition developing the Americans with Disabilities Act.[1]

The building houses an ecumenical community, including the Washington, D.C. offices of the United Methodist Women's Division, the National Council of Churches, the Presbyterian Church (USA), the Episcopal Church, the United Church of Christ, the American Baptist Church and the Mennonite Central Committee.

Over the years, scores of members of Congress have had apartments there, including Newt Gingrich, Max Cleland and the late Albert Gore Sr.

The arrangement has practical results. Rent from the building covered almost a quarter of the General Board of Church and Society's 2000 budget.[2]

It's from this vital ecumenical constellation that United Methodists witness to church and society. They take leading roles in working for legislation to protect the environment, bring debt relief to impoverished countries, curtail the death penalty, address the HIV/AIDS crisis and improve public education.

The Institute on Religion and Democracy (IRD) wants to shut this down. IRD and its allies tried at General Conference 2000. Delegates voted 70 percent to 30 percent not to do so, but IRD is trying again in 2004.

IRD's program fits within the corporate culture that spawned it. Nowhere does IRD express interest in combating poverty, fighting racism, securing health care for the 41 million without health insurance or taking steps to slow global warming.

IRD's *UMAction* newsletter frequently criticizes the board. The newsletter and IRD-related groups consistently refer to it pejoratively as the "political lobby agency." This is akin to saying "all a local pastor does is preach on Sunday."

The prime responsibility of the General Board of Church and Society is to seek the implementation of the Social Principles and other policy statements of the General Conference on Christian social concerns. The agency has a broad program that involves education, advocacy, resource creation and communications. Staff travels throughout the country to meet with United Methodists in local churches and annual conferences. The board's seminar program is host to United Methodist groups from throughout the country who come to the nation's capital to study, reflect and act on social-justice issues.

Its magazine — *Christian Social Action* — has a circulation of 47,000, reaching every United Methodist church in the United States and some in other nations.

The board has a presence at the United Nations, providing the denomination a locus for ministry in the international community.

IRD is working to end all this work.

It sent out a sample resolution in late 2001 calling for shutting down the General Board of Church and Society. Directions for its use were included:

> Consider submitting your resolution to your Annual Conference, your local District's annual meeting, or simply send copies to your bishop and district superintendent.[3]

The sample resolution included half-truths and misstatement. For example:

> • Whereas the Board takes sides on dozens of political issues every year, using the name of our denomination to promote or oppose specific, controversial proposals before the U.S. Congress and the nation;
>
> • Whereas many of the board's positions are not based on the clear commands of Scripture, which should hold the highest authority among United Methodists; and
>
> • Whereas the Board repeatedly goes beyond what is authorized by the UM Social Principles and the resolutions of General Conference, injecting its own slanted political judgment.[4]

In the sample resolution and other publications, IRD fails to note that all board publications and press releases say:

> Only General Conference speaks for the entire denomination. The General Board of Church and Society is the international public policy and social action agency of The United Methodist Church. The board is charged by General Conference with the responsibility of carrying out a program of forthright witness, education and action.[5]

IRD has a self-selecting board. The 63 directors of the General Board of Church and Society are selected through a decentralized process involving all five U.S. geographical jurisdictions and international central conferences.

Eliminating the board would end the United Methodist tradition — the Wesleyan inheritance — of prophetic social witness. Argue with the board. But to allow it to be eliminated would be to surrender Methodist heritage.

UMAction will rally people in annual conferences to offer resolutions that "inflame the church," warned Bishop S. Clifton Ives, General Board of Church and Society president, at a March 2001 meeting. He said:

(IRD's) intent is not reconciliation but division. Do not allow a
force from outside the church to separate you from brothers and
sisters in your conference. Liberals and conservatives must stay
together, must work together, must love and reach out to a hurt-
ing world together.[6]

Bishop Ives' full statement is available on the board's website:
www.umc-gbcs.org. Look under *Christian Social Action,* July-August
2001.

Commissions Are Not Spared
General Commission on the Status and Role of Women

IRD's reform agenda for United Methodists says the church should de-
vote resources to evangelism, discipleship and local-church renewal. To
do this, it claims several existing bodies should be abolished. Among
them is the General Commission on the Status and Role of Women.

The commission, established in 1968, is charged with "working to
achieve the full and equal participation and responsibility of women in
the church." The commission's directors are elected from across the
church and represent a broad diversity of geography, race, ethnicity and
viewpoint.

Its website — www.cosrow.org — describes its work:

Our 42 members wrestle, on behalf of the whole church,
with issues of sexism, the linkages of racism and sexism, inclusive language, and clergy sexual misconduct.... Together,
they work to:

• Foster an awareness of issues, problems and concerns of
women throughout the church;

• Redress inequities in personnel, program, policies and
publications;

• Ensure inclusiveness of women in the total life and mission
of the church in power and policy-making at all levels;

• Empower women to claim responsibility for and take leadership in the mission and ministry of the church.[7]

Eliminating this agency would remove a powerful monitoring body
that keeps the church honest and aware regarding the full inclusion of
women at all levels of the church. It would remove a critical voice for
justice within The United Methodist Church.

General Commission on Religion and Race

The United Methodist Commission on Religion and Race is another vital agency ensuring minority voices are fully expressed, heard and valued in the ministry of the denomination. It was established in 1968. *The Book of Discipline* says:

> The primary purpose is to challenge the general agencies, institutions, and connectional structures of The United Methodist Church to a full and equal participation of the racial and ethnic constituency in the total life and mission of the Church through advocacy and by reviewing and monitoring the practices of the entire Church so as to further ensure racial inclusiveness.[8]

For more on the commission, see its website — www.gcrr.org.

A current commission campaign is to spur the church to take action against sports teams with names and mascots that are demeaning to Native Americans. The campaign, which involves a number of cities and teams, offers one avenue for United Methodists to witness against racial stereotyping.

Mark Tooley, editor of the Institute for Religion and Democracy's *UMAction* newsletter wrote of the campaign:

> As is usually the case on these types of issues, the vast majority of church member have no idea about this campaign [and] have no idea that we even have a church agency called the "Commission on Religion and Race." I'm sure it's not a very effective boycott campaign when their own professed constituency, the United Methodists, is not even aware of the campaign.

The church, however, is aware of the campaign. It is based on legislation that received considerable publicity when passed by the 2000 General Conference meeting in Cleveland, Ohio, during home games of the city's baseball team — the Cleveland Indians. Local and national media carried United Methodist protests of the team's Chief Wahoo mascot.

Tooley said instead of pushing the church to engage in genuine evangelism or applying traditional Christianity to social issues, the Commission on Religion and Race has drifted into liberal politics. He wrote:

> This particular agency is supposed to be an advocate for racial healing and full inclusion of racial minorities within

leadership positions of the [Methodist] Church. But as is often the case, I think this commission falls into the trap of spouting many of the political themes of 'professional' minority groups that specialize in proclaiming their agreed status and advocating quotas and other political causes that tend to be on the left side of the political spectrum.[9]

IRD — not conspicuously in 23 years the champions of any racial or ethnic cause — often claim to speak the mind of "the vast majority of church members." Tooley goes on to imply the Commission on Religion and Race's function is "advocating quotas."

The tactic exposes itself. The quote above slides into implying the commission is "advocating quotas" — a manufactured wedge issue with which to taint it. Clever. Demeaning. But not an argument against the campaign or the commission.

Endnotes

[1] From *GBCS* website: http://wwwumc-gbcs.org/75th-book.htm#1 as appeared 25 March 2003.

[2] Financial Disclosure Report 2000, GBCS.

[3] Tooley, "Sample Resolution for Shutting Down the United Methodist Lobby Office in Washington, D.C."

[4] Ibid.

[5] For an example, see "A Statement on the Iraq War" at http://wwwumc-gbcs.org/news/index.php?newsId=266 as appearing 24 March 2003.

[6] Ives speech.

[7] From http://gcsrw.org/whoweare as appearing 24 March 2003.

[8] From http://wwwgcrr.org/Original%20Web/ministry.htm as appeared 23 March 2003.

[9] Brown ""Methodist Agency on Warpath…."

A Story
What's the Fuss?

Elaine Jacobsen is an 83-year-old United Methodist from Sacramento, California, who has been a member and leader of United Methodist Women and its predecessor organizations at the local, district and conference levels for almost 50 years. She seems an unlikely target of the conservative renewal groups.

But a United Methodist Women circle that Jacobsen and a few other women formed is under attack. And the circle's existence has precipitated attacks against the Women's Division of the United Methodist General Board of Global Ministries because the division hasn't told the circle — known as Sophia Circle — to change its name and study materials.

The Renew Women's Network — a group affiliated with the Good News Movement and UM Action, the United Methodist division of the Institute on Religion and Democracy — has challenged the circle's name and literature its members read. Renew has demanded that the Women's Division either make the circle change its name and stop using material from the *Re-Imagining Newsletter* or force the group to disassociate from United Methodist Women.

Renew sent postcards to those on its mailing list, encouraging them to send the cards on to the Women's Division. The cards read:

> I strongly urge the Women's Division to reconsider the giving of official status to Sophia Circle, whose stated purpose is to meet to study Re-Imagining materials. Re-Imagining

theology is outside the bounds of sound Christian doctrine. The charge to the Women's Division to provide spiritual oversight to the women of the church warrants this action.

Jacobsen had this to say about the charges:

> We have never stated that our purpose is to study Re-Imagining materials. We have simply said we use the section "Can We Talk" from the Re-Imagining community's newsletter as a discussion starter.

She added:

> What are they so afraid of? We pledge to the conference undesignated-giving budget, doubling the pledge last year, and attend district and conference meetings. We participate in schools of Christian mission and the national United Methodist Women assemblies. Many of us are leaders in our local churches, lay members of annual conference, and on district and conference commissions and committees. One was a delegate to General Conference in 1996.

Jacobsen wonders what information Renew is using as the basis for its complaints. No one from Renew has talked to anyone in the circle, she said.

"We would gladly have invited them to attend a meeting to see what was going on," she said.

The story Elaine Jacobsen tells is straightforward. The circle started when Jacobsen and a friend began to attend a monthly one-hour meeting of United Methodist Women at the University of California, Davis Campus. It focused on sections of books, articles and other materials. After a year, the two women decided to replicate the experience in Sacramento.

They invited women from more than one church. This kind of district unit is within established guidelines of United Methodist Women. Jacobsen explained naming the circle:

> When it came time to choose a name, Wisdom/Sophia was suggested. Since *Sophia* is the word for *Wisdom* in the Bible, we decided to use it alone. Additionally, most of us are older and considered that we were *wise*.
>
> After meeting several times, we asked the district United Methodist Women president to charter us as Sophia Circle, Delta District Unit. She agreed. Several district officers attended

the meeting as did two California-Nevada Conference United Methodist Women officers.

Most of us are members of United Methodist Women units in our local United Methodist churches. Our attendance averages 11. We come from seven United Methodist churches. Two women are from a Presbyterian church.

Since we already knew and worked with United Methodist Women materials, we decided to use the *Re-Imagining Newsletter* as a conversation starter. Three of us had attended a Re-Imagining meeting in St. Paul, Minnesota, and found it to be challenging, certainly not frightening or threatening to our core beliefs. We have no formal connection with the Re-Imagining community.

The circle got national attention when a small article about it was published in the *Re-Imagining Newsletter,* Jacobsen said. Her knowledge of the Renew critique is secondhand.

I don't know precisely what Renew has said about us. I have heard that they believe we should be prohibited from using the *Re-Imagining Newsletter* as discussion material. My comment would be that a very wide range of materials is used in small groups across the United Methodist Women's organization. It is not screened by anyone.

I find it hard to understand the fuss. I am stimulated by new ideas, some of which I discard and some of which I incorporate into my life and thinking. That is how we grow, spiritually, mentally, personally.

5
Driving a Wedge

Long ago political strategists identified wedge issues as a tactic of negative political power.

Few have done it as directly as Michael Bauman, professor of theology at Hillsdale College. He put it like this in 1993 at the Ethics and Public Policy Center in Washington, D.C., where the Institute on Religion and Democracy (IRD) stalwart George Weigel is senior fellow:

> The comments that are most successful today are those that are pointed, that are sharp, that are memorable, and that might make your opponent something of a laughing stock....Logical arguments don't very often win the day....It takes rhetorical power and aggressiveness to rally people around your cause.[1]

Wedge issues have roiled U.S. politics for too long. Most work their destructive powers in the broader political culture. Among them are school vouchers, creationism, school prayer, the Ten Commandments, immigration, patriotism.

Their use was relatively rare in mainline church debates until recent decades. Now they are employed regularly by the conservative renewal groups.

What follows is a look at three wedge issues they employ: doctrine, homosexuality and abortion.

Doctrine

- *Orthodox* Christianity,
- *Classical* Christianity,
- *Biblically-based* Christianity,
- *Traditional* Christianity,
- *Wesleyan* theology.

These words are the mantra for doctrinal integrity — a key wedge issue being used especially in the build-up to General Conference 2004.

Groups such as Good News, Renew, the Confessing Movement and IRD express devotion to the "apostolic faith." They claim to be biblically-based and grounded in the ancient creeds. They label opponents as threats to the traditional faith, even heretical. They refuse to engage dialogue. They want opponents forced into compliance or out of the church.

They charge that those who do not articulate theology by their classical definitions:

- Bring about chaos. All Christian doctrine will collapse.
- Do not worship the one true God. Feminists are discredited as "goddess worshipers."
- Are illegitimate Christians because they consider the possibility of more than one way to come to know God.
- Cannot provide safe education for seminarians or teaching and preaching in congregations.

Doctrinal issues are used to stir emotions. Here is how it works. Scott Field, Good News legislative director, told a gathering of United Methodists at the "Confessing the Faith" Conference in Indianapolis Oct. 24, 2002: "It's marvelous that (Bishop Sprague's) book is coming out before Christmas. It will help the cause."

Sprague's January 2002 speech at Iliff School of Theology — taken from a chapter from his book, *Affirmations of a Dissenter* — led 28 conservative renewal movement supporters to file heresy charges against him. (See page 113.)

Good News and the Confessing Movement's doctrinal proposals ignore Methodist history. Methodism has never been unbending in its approach to doctrine. It has supported theological openness and inquiry. Imposing their notion of orthodoxy would send the denomination in a new, rigid direction.

Those who oppose imposition of what conservative renewal groups call "classical Christianity" are charged with disavowing the ancient creeds and United Methodist Articles of Religion. Not true. Those who oppose such a shift treasure these and also value theological exploration, intellectual freedom and God's continuing revelation as crucial components of their faith journey.

Homosexuality

To hear conservative renewal groups tell it, several United Methodist organizations exist solely to promote homosexuality. They've found a tried-and-true wedge issue that stirs emotions while obscuring the real story. Note the common theme in the following quotes from articles found on IRD's website:

- "UM seminary official promotes homosexuality to youth."[2]
- "Ecumenical student conference includes pro-'gay' themes."[3]
- "Pro-homosexuality activists try to portray the success of their cause as inevitable."[4]
- "Still another pro-homosexuality caucus group is represented in *Christian Social Action.*"[5]
- "During the recess, 14 pro-homosexuality Bishops took to the stage to applaud and sing."[6]

Pro-homosexuality seminary officials, activists, caucus groups, bishops — is this all anyone focuses on in The United Methodist Church? These inflammatory statements expose the distortion. A closer look at four of them shows how.

Take the first one. The seminary official who "promoted" homosexuality to youth was in fact encouraging youth to identify their sexual orientation and "claim and name" whatever it might be.

Case 2: It was South African Archbishop Desmond Tutu — anti-apartheid leader and Nobel Peace Prize winner — who was "pro-gay" at the ecumenical student conference. He urged acceptance of "different sexual orientations" and commended the struggle "for justice by gays and lesbians."

Case 3: The "pro-homosexuality caucus" represented in *Christian Social Action* magazine — published by the United Methodist General

Board of Church and Society — is the Methodist Federation for Social Action (MFSA). MFSA has supported human rights for, and church acceptance of, gay men and lesbians for over two decades. It is hardly accurate, however, to describe the broad ministry of this 96-year-old organization as a "pro-homosexuality caucus."

Case 4: It is unlikely even one of the 14 bishops standing on stage at the 2000 General Conference as a witness to their beliefs around inclusiveness would describe themselves as a "pro-homosexuality bishop."

Those who write for the IRD and its *UMAction* newsletter are not careless here. They know what they are doing — using homosexuality as a wedge issue. They create an emotional response to an issue on which Christians differ. To fan the flames, they are deliberately unfair and often disrespectful of those who are their targets.

This tactic is repeated again in an article on IRD's website about the WOW2000 Conference, an ecumenical gathering of Christians who support full inclusion of lesbians and gay men in the church. The closing sentence:

> And many...speakers confirmed the worst fears of many church members that blessing homosexuality would lead to even more dramatic denials of scriptural authority and historic Christian doctrines.[7]

Mainstream Protestant churches have struggled for 25 years to find a way to affirm that Christian gays and lesbians have a place at the altar. Using the issue to discredit churches and their leadership is reprehensible. Lesbians and gay men are "persons of sacred worth."[8] They are not epithets.

Abortion

Recognizing the need for medically safe and legal abortions, The United Methodist Church has supported reproductive choice since 1970. Thousands of women were suffering death or disability from "back-alley" procedures before the Roe-versus-Wade decision of the U.S. Supreme Court. Since 1972, the United Methodist Social Principles have affirmed:

> In continuity with past Christian teaching, we recognize tragic conflicts of life with life that may justify abortion.[9]

Since 1984:

> ...in such cases we support the legal option of abortion un-
> der proper medical procedures.[10]

Lifewatch and other conservative renewal groups with increasing success have used abortion as a wedge issue. The 2000 General Conference added:

> We oppose the use of late-term abortion known as dilations
> and extraction (partial-birth abortion)....[11]

Lifewatch and its supporters have labeled those who support a woman's right to make her own choices about a pregnancy "pro-abortion." They have created division and stirred heated debate where thoughtful discussion would serve all involved better.[12]

This is illustrated in the September 2000 *Lifewatch* newsletter. Reporting the 2000 addition on late-term abortions:

> First, by opposing partial-birth abortion, The United Metho-
> dist Church breaks ranks with the pro-choice/pro-abortion
> political lobby. Before this legislation against partial-birth
> abortion was passed by General Conference, The United
> Methodist Church had been officially and unquestionably
> pro-choice on abortion, for decades, and silent on the par-
> tial-birth procedure. *The Book of Discipline's* pro-choice
> paragraph and its silence on partial-birth abortion allowed
> United Methodist leaders and general-church boards to sup-
> port political lobbies which are sustaining the legality of all
> abortion, including this particularly repulsive form of late-
> term abortion.
>
> In this way, certain United Methodist leaders and boards
> provided religious cover, religious legitimization, to those
> who are maintaining the legal status of partial-birth abor-
> tion. Therefore, certain United Methodist leaders and insti-
> tutions directly collaborated with the Culture of Death.
>
> However, now that the anti-partial-birth-abortion lan-
> guage has been added to the *Discipline,* The United Metho-
> dist Church is no longer a partial-birth-abortion collabora-
> tor. Therefore, The United Methodist Church officially op-
> poses what, a matter of months ago, she was supporting —
> the radical, pro-choice/pro-abortion political lobby.[13]

Several things stand out:

- The term *partial-birth abortion* is political. There is no medical procedure by this name. The procedure referred to — medically known as dilation and extraction — is rarely performed.
- The claim that The United Methodist Church supported "the radical, pro-choice/pro-abortion political lobby" is woven throughout the article. According to *Lifewatch,* the church was a "partial-birth-abortion collaborator." Such allegations ignore the church's compassionate, faithful statement on abortion before 2000.
- The claim that "certain United Methodist leaders and institutions directly collaborated with the Culture of Death" is ominous. But which leaders? And what is a "culture of death"?

The article also claims:

> By opposing partial-birth abortion, The United Methodist Church shows that she is able to overcome the maneuverings of the small but well-organized pro-choice/pro-abortion minority within the denomination.[14]

Lifewatch uses inaccurate and emotionally-laden terms. And it claims to speak for the majority of United Methodists — a tactic that cuts across conservative renewal groups.

The official position of The United Methodist Church on abortion is found in the Social Principles. It is worth printing because it demonstrates a depth hard to caricature:

> Abortion — The beginning of life and the ending of life are the God-given boundaries of human existence. While individuals have always had some degree of control over when they would die, they now have the awesome power to determine when and even whether new individuals will be born.
>
> Our belief in the sanctity of unborn human life makes us reluctant to approve abortion. But we are equally bound to respect the sacredness of the life and well-being of the mother, for whom devastating damage may result from an unacceptable pregnancy. In continuity with past Christian teaching, we recognize tragic conflicts of life with life that may justify abortion, and in such cases we support the legal option of abortion under proper medical procedures.

We cannot affirm abortion as an acceptable means of birth control, and we unconditionally reject it as a means of gender selection. We oppose the use of late-term abortion known as dilatation and extraction (partial-birth abortion) and call for the end of this practice except when the physical life of the mother is in danger and no other medical procedure is available, or in the case of severe fetal anomalies incompatible with life.

We call all Christians to a searching and prayerful inquiry into the sorts of conditions that may warrant abortion. We commit our Church to continue to provide nurturing ministries to those who terminate a pregnancy, to those in the midst of a crisis pregnancy, and to those who give birth.

Governmental laws and regulations do not provide all the guidance required by the informed Christian conscience. Therefore, a decision concerning abortion should be made only after thoughtful and prayerful consideration by the parties involved, with medical, pastoral, and other appropriate counsel.[15]

Endnotes

[1] Cromartie and Kristol *Disciples and Democracy.*
[2] Nelson "UM Seminary…."
[3] *UMAction* "Ecumenical Student Conference…."
[4] Tooley "Mainline Churches Ever Firmer…" quoting Diane Knippers.
[5] IRD "UM Finance Agency…."
[6] *UMAction* "UM General Conference…."
[7] *UMAction* "Pro-'Gay' Mainline Church Caucus Groups Rally."
[8] *The Book of Discipline, 2000* ¶161[G].
[9] *The Book of Discipline 1984, 1988, 1992, 1996, 2000.*
[10] *The Book of Discipline 1984, 1988, 1992, 1996, 2000.*
[11] *The Book of Discipline, 2000* ¶161 (J).
[12] Lifewatch flyer, Lifewatch and Renew flyer.
[13] Stallsworth.
[14] Ibid.
[15] *The Book of Discipline, 2000* ¶161 (J).

6
The Right and Race

As this book went to press, the U.S. Supreme Court heard the most important affirmative action case in 25 years. The suit challenged the University of Michigan's effort to recruit a representative student body for undergraduate and law-school education.

The case drew a remarkable amount of response in the media and public discourse. Unexpectedly several establishment groups — CEOs of giant corporations and several retired generals and former heads of military academies — filed briefs supporting Michigan. An integrated executive suite or officer corps is essential, they argued. The only way to assure that is through affirmative action.[1]

Support for affirmative action is not a given these days. The political landscape is crowded with people and groups working to curtail programs — in schools, in employment, in business — that try to compensate for decades of racial and gender discrimination. Almost every right-wing think tank has a hand in discrediting affirmative action.

Back in 1981, 10 days after President Reagan took office, the powerful Heritage Foundation issued a 3,000-page "Mandate for Leadership." Much of it became part of Reagan's agenda. It called for "colorblind" policies, a "neutral" Justice Department, and revocation of orders favoring minority government hiring and contracting. That did not happen wholesale. But it led the way for narrowing of such opportunities.

Racial profiling by police — facing serious court challenges before 9/11 — is now being justified as necessary for homeland security. It is only one example of a rise in racist behavior in the current climate of fear.

When Ralph Reed was turning the Christian Coalition into a political force, he talked about a diverse community:

> There's no question that white evangelical Protestants, especially in the South, were not only on the sidelines but were on the wrong side of the most central struggle for social justice of the 20th century, namely the struggle for civil rights.[2]

In 2002 as head of Georgia's Republican Party, Reed may have stepped back into a past he criticized. His party used the Confederate flag — an historic wedge issue — to divide the races in the 2002 gubernatorial campaign.

The white evangelical Protestants that Reed refers to certainly have no corner on racism. The United Methodist Church, despite several earnest efforts, often has failed to acknowledge and work against injustices that harm people of color in church and society.

What of the conservative renewal groups being explored in this book? Their failure to take seriously the evil of racism is reflected less in what they say and do and more in what they don't say and don't do.

The 2004 General Conference agenda of Good News and related groups lists issues in priority order, said Scott Field, Good News legislative director. Racial reconciliation is listed last among their concerns. The one suggested petition calls for a pulpit exchange on or near Dr. Martin Luther King Jr.'s birthday.

At the 2002 "Confessing the Faith" Conference in Indianapolis, Field advocated building alliances with people of color to broaden the appeal of the renewal agenda. Such alliances would also prevent conservative renewal groups from being accused of not caring about racial-justice issues.

The virtual silence of conservative renewal groups on issues of racial justice suggests their leaders do not envision the potential richness of a multiethnic community, or at the very least, it is not a high priority.

Thankfully, we have leaders in The United Methodist Church who have a far different vision. Working through such vehicles as the ethnic caucuses, the General Commission on Religion and Race, and United

Methodists of Color for a Fully Inclusive Church, they aid the church in keeping its eyes on the prize. They point to the fullness of God's creation in all its racial and ethnic diversity.

Gilbert H. Caldwell, a former district superintendent now retired in Denver, Colo., shares his perspective on African Americans' involvement in the church:

> Hymn No. 519 in our *United Methodist Hymnal* has these words in the second stanza: 'We have come over a way that with tears has been watered; we have come, treading our path through the blood of the slaughtered.'
>
> Inclusion of "Lift Every Voice and Sing" in our hymnal recognizes the survival and accomplishment of persons of African descent in The United Methodist Church and in larger society.
>
> Those in The United Methodist Church who oppose affirmative action illustrate lack of awareness of or insensitivity to the history and continuing struggles of descendants of an African people 'imported' to North America to provide free slave labor. Some assume individual successes of gifted Black persons in our denomination and in society indicate that the battle for racial justice is over. They fail to comprehend the continuing gaps that exist in our nation. We live in a culture that embraces Black super stars while ignoring the continuing needs of many persons in the communities from whence stars emerge.
>
> The United Methodist Church has been blessed to have in its membership hundreds of African Americans who have led in the transformation of both our denomination and our nation.
>
> What blessing has been showered on the church by people like: Cain Felder, Dorothy Height, Theressa Hoover, Bishop Leontine Kelly, James Lawson, Joseph Lowery, Randolph Nugent, Bishop Melvin Talbert, Bishop James Thomas, Barbara Ricks Thompson, Bishop Woodie White, Cecil Williams. These are just 11 of the hundreds of names that could be mentioned.
>
> If some persons of vision had not been concerned about the absence of Black leadership in the church — and had not

known of the significant gifts of those listed above — The United Methodist Church would have been diminished. It would have been deprived of the talent of persons molded and shaped by the distinctively different experience of Americans who trace their roots to the African continent.

African Americans have brought to the American experience their sense of history, heritage and hope. Those who resist efforts to intentionally include those who have a direct link to that history deprive us all.

Endnotes

[1] Greenhouse Sec. 4:4.
[2] Martin 360.

7
The Wider Picture: We're Not Alone

The United Methodist Church is not alone in facing the challenges described in this study. The Presbyterian Church (USA) and the Episcopal Church, USA, have also seen conservative renewal movements emerge in recent decades with similar infrastructures, publications, rhetoric and wedge-issue legislative strategies. And the leadership of the Southern Baptist Convention has been taken over by ultra-conservatives.

These movements, which have begun to work together across denominational lines, are operating in a broadening context of religious change that is increasingly intertwined with political and social change. How did the present situation develop?

The conflicts roiling the mainline churches bear some resemblance to the fundamentalist controversies of the early 20th century, when the wedge issue was Darwinian evolution. Today's fundamentalist backlash, while intellectually rooted in earlier controversies over biblical authority and interpretation, is much more explicitly tied to right-wing political trends and social-policy agendas.

The correlation of mainline evangelical renewal with the rise of the New Right is plain to see. For example, the Institute on Religion and Democracy's four-year "Reforming America's Churches" plan for 2001-2004, is a roadmap for using mainline religious institutions to shape wider policy goals. The opening paragraph of the document says:

Conservatives have won surprising victories on key theological and sexuality issues at recent church conventions. Now is the time to translate those victories into real influence for conservatives within the permanent governing structures of these churches, *so they can help renew the wider culture of our nation* (emphasis added).[1]

The document goes on to list a host of the Institute on Religion and Democracy (IRD) ultra-conservative social-policy goals. A few include:
• Increasing militarism,
• Opposing environmental protection efforts,
• Eliminating social programs, and
• Resisting hate-crime legislation.

These objectives have a greater chance of succeeding if religious opposition to them is weakened by factional strife and destabilization within mainline churches — the *modus operandi* of groups like IRD and the denominational groups related to it.

Alarming as these tactics may be, historical perspective is crucial to understanding the conviction, long-term vision and trans-denominational character of the contemporary conservative resurgence in mainline churches.

Beginning with the Presbyterians

It is not surprising that the Presbyterian Church (USA) was the first to see a conservative renewal movement emerge in the mid-1960s. Presbyterianism had challenged fundamentalist power politics with its 1924 Auburn Affirmation. That served as a rallying point for theological pluralism in the face of a major fundamentalist campaign to introduce strict theological tests for ordination and employment within the church. After World War II, moderate and liberal forces were led by a new generation of pastors and leaders trained in historical and critical biblical-interpretation methods.

The story was repeated in other mainline traditions. With the post-World War II economic boom, these churches grew significantly in membership and assets, becoming an important component of the white middle- and upper-class establishments. The founding of the National Council of Churches in 1950 was one important point in a process where mainline social witness began its reign as the dominant religious perspective in public life. It was a time of critical social progress spearheaded by the rise of the Civil Rights Movement.[2]

Many conservatives — Good News founder Charles Keysor called them the "silent minority" — stayed within mainline churches despite the shifting intellectual tide in their pastorates and national structures.

It is clear that three mainline churches — Methodist, Episcopal and Presbyterian — made a significant mark on national life after World War II by putting their financial and theological weight behind social progress.[3]

As the visibility and energy of progressive causes — civil rights, women's rights, the anti-war movement, Third World solidarity movements — grew in the mid-1960s, the churches' support for such causes became a red flag for social conservatives, mainly businessmen, in their midst.

Growing Opposition

While out of power in most of the official mainline structures, the men who started the mainline conservative renewal movements were prime beneficiaries of a dominant social establishment — white, male and corporate — that to them seemed increasingly in question as pressures for equality and justice grew.

As the churches ceased to be a source of legitimacy for the social power and class interests challenged by these movements, a counter-mobilization was organized. Shadow structures like the United Methodist Good News and the Presbyterian Lay Committee were created to give voice to conservative social interests and to speak out against official agencies and leadership, which they thought had captured the church for ungodly causes and reasons.

Although mainline renewal movements have progressed at varying rates and with varying levels of influence and success, the structures, methods, rhetoric and theological claims of these movements are similar in each denomination. This suggests a trans-denominational character that goes beyond historic controversies and confessional boundaries, opening onto a much wider vista of religious change in the United States.

A struggle for control of mainline Protestantism — its assets, power and heritage — is unfolding on a trans-denominational basis today. The mainline churches' ability to engage and respond to the profound challenges faced by the U.S. mainstream in this time of deepening social inequality, retrenchment against civil liberties and civil rights, and looming disintegration of international order, is very much at stake.

Presbyterian Lay Committee — and More

The Presbyterian conservative renewal movement is the wealthiest and most comprehensive, reflecting the denomination's relatively greater wealth and its legacy as a religious home for business leaders and political elites. The central organization, analogous to Good News in The United Methodist Church, is the Presbyterian Lay Committee, which was founded in 1965 by J. Howard Pew, scion of the Sun Oil empire.

The Presbyterian Lay Committee has roughly twice the resources of Good News, with a budget of approximately $2 million in 2000 and more than $4 million in assets.[4] Its main publication, *The Presbyterian Layman,* has a circulation of nearly 600,000, making it the most widely distributed Presbyterian publication in the world. It received $187,500 a year from the Pew Memorial Trusts long after J. Howard Pew's death in what is known by insiders as a "historic family interest." More than $4 million came in from Pew from 1968-1996.

The total annual income of conservative renewal organizations active in denominational politics within the Presbyterian Church (USA) in 2000 was approximately $7.9 million. This figure would be much higher if it included the income of mission organizations connected to the renewal movement. Like The Mission Society for United Methodists, these organizations operate outside official mission structures but draw heavily from church members for financial support. In contrast, progressive advocacy groups in the Presbyterian Church (USA) took in approximately $600,000 in 2000.[5]

In both The United Methodist and Presbyterian churches, issue-based organizations have emerged around the main conservative renewal institution, focused on abortion, homosexuality and feminism. In the Presbyterian Church (USA), organizations have emerged on evangelical church growth and seminary renewal, charismatic renewal, orthodox theological scholarship, and web-based strategic resourcing.

As in The United Methodist Church, the Presbyterian conservative renewal movement focused on enacting and defending a constitutional ban on gay/lesbian ordination in the 1990s. As a wedge issue, this success has had a deep effect on the church. It has given conservatives leverage to push for what they define as "constitutional integrity," requiring judicial action against those deemed to be in violation of church law.

This has created a juridical atmosphere within the church rife with division and fear. This climate has precipitated calls for new mechanisms of constitutional and theological accountability and polity reforms to enhance the conservative thrust within the church. In The United Methodist Church, the Coalition for United Methodist Accountability — founded in 2000 by Good News, the Confessing Movement, and the Institute on Religion and Democracy — represents a similar trend.

Demeaning Leaders

In both United Methodist and Presbyterian churches, attacks on church officials and agencies have had an impact. They continue to weaken the churches' historic efforts to support the work of national boards, women's work and theological discourse. This diminishes a strong public witness promoting peace, equality and justice in national life.

While not comprising a takeover in the way the Southern Baptist Convention was taken over (see below), the effects of this decades-long bombardment is felt in organizational change and attrition in structure, finances, policy and personnel.

Instead of taking over agencies and institutions, the mainline conservative renewal strategy is to attack church offices and personnel who represent more progressive viewpoints calling for their defunding, dissolution or defrocking. UM Action's current demand for elimination of The United Methodist Church's General Board of Church and Society, Commission on the Status and Role of Women, and Commission on Religion and Race, and the Good News/Renew call for changes in United Methodist Women/Women's Division are indicative of this trend.

Legislative Strategy

In recent years, mainline churches have seen their national legislative bodies increasingly politicized by well-financed conservative "war rooms" that far outstrip the finances of their counterparts on the other side. The goal is to gain control of church structures.

Signs of conservatives' political planning and action in keeping with this trend were evident at the 2000 General Conference of The United Methodist Church in Cleveland, Ohio:

• Judicial Council elections saw conservatives affiliated with the conservative renewal movement gain three seats;
• Conservatives were added to the University Senate, the body that accredits colleges, universities and seminaries; and
• A major polity reform, reapportioned delegate strength to the Southeastern and South Central jurisdictions based on membership trends.

Key in these matters is institutional power and how it overlaps with social power. At Good News' beginning, founder and magazine editor Charles Keysor, its board of directors, and its supporters did not seek schism, overturning of leadership or replacing of the power dynamics. "A voice" for those not represented in the major dynamics of The United Methodist Church was the goal. Later, disillusioned with the failure of the movement to enter the core identity of the denomination, Keysor left The United Methodist Church. Small steps leading to potentially larger results, however, had begun to develop. A few of those alternative expressions:

• A mission-sending organization,
• Confirmation materials, and
• A women's organization.

When issues around homosexuality began to take center stage, more and more voices were heard from within the Good News movement urging a formal separation of those who believed their position was a minority voice.

Some pastors did leave. Talk arose about "a split in the church" in the mid-1990s. Progressive voices from within urged the others to remain, believing dialogue and struggle together could accomplish a common viewpoint. Some significant public symbolic actions — same-gender holy unions, appointments of gay or lesbian clergy, and "coming out" of lesbian and gay clergy — catalyzed persons on both sides of the issue.

By 2000, as more General Conference delegates began to vote Good News positions, the conservative renewal message changed. On a video produced by Good News before the 2000 General Conference, Good

News legislative director Scott Field said:

> Those people who feel they cannot live within the covenant
> of United Methodism should be allowed and encouraged to
> leave without penalty. Only delegates to General Conference
> will be able to make this a reality. Parties are kept together
> largely because of property, apportionments and pensions.[6]

This change was not only a matter of controlling the theological agenda
of the church, but also its resources, and not only at the national level.
Recent efforts by Thomas C. Oden, Institute on Religion and Democracy chair and leader in the Confessing Movement, are an indication.
He has linked the trust clause central to ownership of United Methodist
property to "doctrinal" fidelity. His long-term goal is to use civil-court
challenges to deprive local congregations of their buildings and their
holdings unless they embrace his conservative views. His massive es-
say on this subject is posted on the Good News website.

Episcopal Church Pressures

The conservative renewal groups are not simply theological movements in inspiration, methods or public goals.

With deep roots in the historic evangelical revival movement within
the wider Anglican church, the Episcopal conservative renewal movement has an institutional history somewhat different from that of
United Methodist and Presbyterian churches. It wasn't until 1996 that
the American Anglican Council, the national organization representing
conservative objectives within the Episcopal Church, USA, was
formed. In six years, the council — founded in Texas but now based in
Washington, D.C. — has grown and, like Good News, has an annual income of approximately $1 million. IRD President Diane Knippers is a
major player in the council.

Although homosexuality is the key wedge issue for the Episcopal
movement, as it is in United Methodist and Presbyterian churches, no
constitutional ban on gay ordination has been enacted. Most commenta-
tors argue that Episcopal conservatives have made little national legislative headway compared to their counterparts in other mainline
churches. But the global structure of Anglicanism has provided avenues
for U.S. Episcopal conservatives to attack the church in other ways.

The strategy is to use mechanisms of the church's "Global Communion" to challenge and destabilize the U.S. church's ecclesial status. This has taken on a schismatic thrust with the recent formation of the Anglican Mission in America, which provides conservative leaders and parishes with alternative jurisdiction under the authority of conservative bishops overseas.

Many of the leaders and parishes drawn to the Anglican Mission in America are seeking protection from church laws requiring women's ordination. The organization sees the United States as a "mission field." This provides alternative jurisdiction for conservative U.S. Episcopal priests — some of whom have been consecrated as Anglican Mission in America bishops as a form of church planting for new Anglican churches.[7]

Southern Baptist Takeover

Although by no means a perfect analogy, it is instructive to understand what has happened to the Southern Baptist Convention and how the wider religious right perceives the mainline conservative renewal movements, to grasp better the political character of these movements.

Although not a liberal church to begin with, guided historically by a strong pietistic mind-set that generally eschewed politics, the Southern Baptist Convention has suffered the most pervasive and politically acute conservative challenge. It was taken over from the top in the 1980s. Purges, schisms and acknowledged right-wing loyalties have followed.

C. Welton Gaddy, former Southern Baptist Convention leader and now executive director of the Interfaith Alliance, describes the Southern Baptist Convention takeover this way:

> In 1978, Judge Paul Pressler and the Rev. Paige Patterson announced a 10-year plan to transform the Southern Baptist Convention by means of establishing fundamentalists' control of all of its boards and agencies. A few of us who were members of the Southern Baptist Convention at that time took the threat seriously and planned to counter the fundamentalists' efforts at a takeover. Unfortunately, far more, including many of the convention's elected leaders, dismissed the Pressler-Patterson plan as just another passing comment by a group of disgruntled people. The Southern Baptist Convention was lost to the religious right as much because of mainline Baptists' refusal to take seriously and counter a re-

ligious right threat as because of the leaders and strategies of the takeover movement. I would hope that leaders in other denominations learned from what transpired in the Southern Baptist Convention.[8]

One lesson learned is that language matters. Kenneth Chafin, purged by the Southern Baptist Convention fundamentalist leadership from his post as Billy Graham professor of evangelism and Carl Bates professor of preaching at Southwestern Baptist Theological Seminary in Fort Worth, Texas, emphasizes the use of language, rhetoric and symbolism by the takeover leaders:

> In the past, they worked hard to convince people that the controversy was about the Bible. They gathered followers who had been told that they were 'shaping a new theology.' But the truth is now evident; the movement was more about a grab for power than the emergence of a new theology. It was more about imposing a 'mind-set' than leading more people to experience God's freedom. It was more about excluding all who disagreed with them than finding a basis of unity in Christ. The proof of this conclusion is evident from what they did once they gained control.[9]

Despite striking similarities in rhetorical strategy and targeting — most notably of women's leadership — understanding the Southern Baptist Convention takeover does not necessarily provide a roadmap for what is happening in The United Methodist Church and other mainline churches. The Southern Baptist Convention has a more conservative membership and a polity that, while highly decentralized, is paradoxically susceptible to top-down takeover. Appointment powers are lodged in the convention's presidency. Fundamentalists won that consistently in the 1980s and 1990s.

The Religious Right Takes Notice

With the takeover of the Southern Baptist Convention, the wider religious right has begun to focus on historic religious institutions like the Southern Baptist Convention and the mainline Protestant churches as potential allies in their prosecution of the culture wars. James C. Dobson's $120 million para-church service and media empire, Focus on the Family, began to work closely with Southern Baptist Convention leadership in the 1990s while also turning its attention to the mainline churches. In October 1998, for example, Focus on the Family's public-affairs magazine *Citizen* ran a feature titled "Pulling the Mainline Back in Line: Renewal Groups are Working Hard to Return Mainline Churches to their Scriptural Foundations."

One example where mainline leaders are working closely with the religious right is the Alliance for Marriage. This organization even enjoyed a brief endorsement from the National Council of Churches before that approval was hastily withdrawn. It has developed a federal constitutional amendment that prohibits legal protections for same-sex marriage.

The alliance networks through an advisory board that reads like a who's who of mainline conservative renewal, including James V. Heidinger II, president of Good News.[10] The amendment was co-authored by Princeton University jurisprudence professor Robert George, a board member of the Institute on Religion and Democracy and an important legal theorist of the religious right.

While using the language of theology to carry their causes forward, the agendas of conservative renewal groups across denominations are linked with far broader right-wing forces in the society. These movements are not merely about reform. They are about power and control. They are not simply about remaking the church. They are carefully crafted tools of those who would reshape the wider culture to their vision.

Endnotes

[1] Institute on Religion and Democracy's "Reforming America's Churches Project 2001-2004, Executive Summary" 1.

[2] Findlay 11ff. In 1958 President Eisenhower himself laid the cornerstone for the Interchurch Center at 475 Riverside Drive in New York City, the headquarters of the National Council of Churches and for decades thereafter the national hub of mainline social-justice activities.

[3] Read against the grain, United Methodist IRD leader Edmund Robb's 1986 screed *Betrayal of the Church* provides a useful window onto mainline social-justice activities.

[4] Presbyterian Lay Committee, IRS Form 990: 2000.

[5] Daly "Power and Politics" 194.

[6] Field UM Decision 2000.

[7] For a more detailed analysis of the AMIA and other aspects of the Episcopal Church, USA, renewal movement, see Daly, "A Church at Risk: The Episcopal 'Renewal Movement'."

[8] Gaddy.

[9] Kenneth Chapin from Kell and Camp in *In The Name of the Father*...xi. This fine study of the rhetorical strategies of the Southern Baptist Convention fundamentalists regarding biblical authority, the role of the women in the church, homosexuality, and other issues, reveals striking overlaps with the mainline situation and should be studied for the lessons it holds about the importance of language in generating institutional change.

[10] See the *Alliance for Marriage* website at www.allianceformarriage.org.

8
Funding a Movement:
The War of Ideas

The activities in the churches described in this book reflect and gain energy from developments in the broad U.S. culture over the last quarter of the 20th century. During that time, conservative voices — amplified by hundreds of millions of dollars in corporate donations — played a major role in framing the political debate.

That led to the rise of the New Right and Religious Right, the most important story in U.S. politics during that period.

The Religious Right emerged from a half-century of political absence — roughly 1925-1975 — to claim "a place at the table in this conversation we call democracy" — a phrase often used by former Christian Coalition President Ralph Reed.[1] The New Right grew out of the 1964 Goldwater rebellion against Eastern and Midwestern establishment Republicanism.

Evangelicals helped elect "born-again" Jimmy Carter in 1976. Both the New and Religious Right were important to Ronald Reagan's election in 1980. Together they fueled the Newt Gingrich congressional revolution of 1994.

Forty-six percent of Americans identified themselves as evangelicals or born-again Christians in a December 2002 Gallup Poll. They have hit political pay-dirt in the presidency of George W. Bush. Here's what *Newsweek* said in March 2003:

> As a subaltern in his father's 1988 campaign, George Bush

the Younger assembled his career through contacts with ministers of the then emerging evangelical movement in political life. Now they form the core of the Republican Party, which controls all of the capital for the first time in a half century. Bible-believing Christians are Bush's strongest backers, and turning them out next year in even greater numbers is the top priority of the president's political adviser Karl Rove. He is busy tending to the base with pro-life judicial appointments, a proposed ban on human cloning (approved by the House last week) and a $15 billion plan to fight AIDS in Africa, a favorite project of Christian missionaries.... The base is returning the favor. They are, by far, the strongest supporters of a war — unilateral if need be — to remove Saddam.[2]

Conservative Christians increasingly were unwilling to focus only on the spiritual in their houses of worship when so much was going on in the society that disturbed them.

Increasingly they responded to calls to express themselves politically. Jerry Falwell was an example of the change. In 1979, he created the Moral Majority — it lasted a decade — to make a political impact. Just a decade earlier, Falwell had said in a sermon that it was his job to save souls, not act politically.[3]

Some aspects of the emergence of a variety of conservative political and religious expressions in the last 30 years are well-known. Look at the 1990s impact of the Christian Coalition — now struggling. Observe how common Rush Limbaugh-style talk radio has become. Megabucks media-magnet Rupert Murdoch has put his impact on Fox television, several newspapers and a publishing house and founded *The Weekly Standard,* a neoconservative political magazine edited by William Kristol. Fred Barnes, who joined IRD's board in 2003, is No. 2 to Kristol.

Other developments are not public knowledge, such as the strategic creation of hundreds of conservative think tanks and advocacy groups through the generous provision of money by conservative secular foundations and corporations.

It is important for engaged citizens to know this story. Otherwise, the information necessary to respond in our communities, in our institutions, in our churches, in our ballots is not available.

The right of people to express their political or religious sentiments is not the issue, but the dimensions of this story, the style of attack, the sources and amounts of the funds do raise serious questions.

Ideas

The resurgence of the new Political Right was not a coincidence. Corporations and foundations decided to put their money where their interests were. People like William E. Simon, treasury secretary under President Gerald Ford and President Richard Nixon and former Marxist political guru Irving Kristol, William Kristol's father, played visionary roles.

Noting that corporations exist to make a profit, they appealed for "businessmen (to) give the same kind of careful thought to their corporate contributions as they do their capital investments."[4]

Irving Kristol identified a tactic in his *Wall Street Journal* column that has been widely used: Attack the integrity, not the words, of those with whom you disagree.[5]

His advice was heeded. Money cascaded in, finding new repositories. Total *foundation* funding to only 20 key center-right and far-right think tanks and advocacy groups exceeded an astounding $1 billion during the 1990s.[6]

Beyond foundation money, at least as much corporate and wealthy individual money also has poured into right-wing movements. The battle cries became "culture wars" or "war of ideas."

James C. Dobson, head of the rich and powerful Focus on the Family, and Gary Bauer, Religious Right candidate for the Republican presidential nomination in 2000, defined the stakes aggressively in 1990 in their widely read book, *Children at Risk: The Battle for the Hearts and Minds of Our Children:*

> Nothing short of a great Civil War of Values rages today
> throughout North America. Two sides with vastly differing
> and incompatible worldviews are locked in a bitter conflict
> that permeates every level of society. Instead of fighting for
> territory or military conquest, however, the struggle now is
> for the hearts and minds of people. It is a war over ideas.

Foundation and corporate funds were crucial to address those issues for which money was not freely available. Middle- and-working-class people are likely to give to causes that cut close to them: opposing gay rights and immigration, supporting prayer in school, and limiting abortion. But tort reform, deregulation, monitoring the courts and constructing alternative media depend on special income. A lot of the money was given unrestricted — not a foundation tradition.

Those are important innovations. The Institute for Policy Studies, one of the few multi-issue institutions on the left, had a 2001 budget of $1.5 million.[7] That would run the powerful right-wing Heritage Foundation for only three weeks.

The first law of political success is to define the debate. The groups created or energized by this money do research, make recommendations, and push their concepts into the public debate by vigorous use of the media, energizing a constituency and cultivating politicians.

The Heritage Foundation is a model. Over 30 years it has used scads of money — a budget of $31 million in 2003 — to collect very smart people to push very conservative ideas very effectively — at times ruthlessly.[8] They joined other major advocacy think tanks like the American Enterprise Institute, Cato Institute and Hudson Institute.

In time, 300 other conservative advocacy institutions followed, some in Washington, D.C., as are those just cited, many in state capitals. The 2001 tax cuts favoring the richest Americans would not have happened without them. Privatizing Medicare and Social Security emerged from these think tanks. So did the North American Free Trade Agreement and missile-shield defense systems and, long before 9/11, the concept of targeting Iraq.

They work across the spectrum, making an impact electorally, legislatively, in the courts. Notice how often Jay Sekulow appears in the news. He heads Pat Robertson's American Center for Law and Justice and litigates often on religious-freedom cases from the right. They are cited thousands of times a year in news stories, rarely identified as anything other than presumed experts.[9]

Hand it to them. The architects of this conservative resurgence have outworked, outspent, out-thought and out-organized their progressive counterparts. No equivalent commitment to create ideological outposts or shape a political agenda exists on the part of centrist and progressive foundations or corporations.

Take one clear example of the gap between the two. *Extra,* the magazine of Fairness and Accuracy in Reporting, did a study of think-tank media citations in 2000. Conservative think tanks were quoted 11,107 times in major media. Progressive think tanks had 4,471 citations.[10]

Money

Look at six key sources of funds for the conservative groups. Begin with Richard Mellon Scaife, so valued for supporting the right he has been called "the funding father."

The 70-year-old Pittsburgh-based billionaire is the scion of bank and oil money made by his great-grandfather, Thomas Mellon. Between 1965 and 1998, his foundations — Sarah Mellon Scaife, Allegheny and Carthage — gave at least $340 million to conservative causes and institutions — about $620 million in 1999 dollars, adjusted for inflation.[11]

Much larger foundations — Ford, Rockefeller, Lilly, Pew — give away a lot more money to a broad range of causes. But as *The Washington Post* — from whose data base the above figures came — said in an extensive profile of Scaife in 1999:

> By concentrating his giving on a specific ideological objective for nearly 40 years, and making most of his grants with no strings attached, Scaife's philanthropy has had a disproportionate impact on the rise of the right....[12]

Scaife may be the premier player, but he is not alone in conservative largesse. Three others worked so closely with the Scaife foundations that they were dubbed the "four sisters." They were also rated by one monitor as four of the five most conservative foundations in the United States.

One is the John M. Olin Foundation with offices in New York City. Olin Chemical owns Winchester Rifles and produces chemicals, copper and much more. The foundation became the leader in focused ideological giving when William E. Simon became president. Following the wishes of the late John Olin, the foundation is now spending down its money. Deregulation is a key issue for Olin.

Another is the Lynde and Harry Bradley Foundation, based in Milwaukee, Wisconsin. The brothers made a fortune in electronics and expressed their politics by belonging to the far-right John Birch Society. School vouchers have been Bradleys' special cause.[13]

The fourth "sister" was Smith Richardson Foundation with North

Carolina roots and money from Vicks products, augmented later by such products as Nyquil and Clearasil. In the last few years, this foundation has changed its orientation and is no longer a sister.[14]

Several other foundations still play the game. One is Castle Rock, created from the Adolph Coors Foundation in 1993. Coors founded the Coors beer empire.

Another is the California-based Fieldstead Foundation, the conduit for the interests of Howard Fieldstead Ahmanson, whose father amassed a fortune in the savings-and-loan industry. Ahmanson has had a major impact on California politics for his support of anti-gay rights, anti-choice, anti-immigration, anti-union, pro school-voucher and pro school-prayer movements.[15] His wife, Roberta Green Ahmanson, is on the Insitute for Religion and Democracy Board (IRD) of Directors.

As Peter Steinfels, now a religion columnist at *The New York Times,* put it more than 20 years ago, such developments as the addition of a religious emphasis at the secular American Enterprise Institute and the birth of IRD came out of the intersection of fundamentalism and right-wing politics. He wrote:

> The IRD is part of an obviously larger movement in American politics and culture, the growth of a network of intellectual institutions that function to dampen outbreaks of fundamental social criticism.[16]

IRD publishes the *UMAction* newsletter. IRD's published priorities are to focus on the Episcopal, Presbyterian and United Methodist denominations. The results are systemic attacks on individuals and attempts to undermine leaders and agencies of churches.

IRD received about $4.4 million in secular ideological funding from its founding in 1981 through 2001, almost all of that from the six foundations just described.[17]

Ernest LeFever founded the Ethics and Public Policy Center with much the same money. He issued strong attacks on the World and National Councils of Churches. In 1981, he failed to receive Senate confirmation to be the human-rights staff person at the U.S. State Department. He had covered-up secret donations to his center from the Nestle Corporation to defend Nestle against charges that its infant formula was hazardous in Third-World settings.[18]

Richard John Neuhaus — first a Lutheran pastor and now a Roman

Catholic priest — runs the Institute on Religion and Public Life. He created it in 1989 with $100,000 from Scaife. Through 2001, the institute had received $7,387,500 from conservative foundations, primarily the Scaife set, Bradley, Castle Rock and Olin.[19] Neuhaus, credited as the primary drafter of IRD's foundation document, "Christianity and Democracy" — still available on the IRD website — may have presaged the IRD style of invective. He said on "60 Minutes" in 1983, "What worries me most is when the church starts telling lies."[20]

Another IRD founder, Michael Novak, heads a program at the American Enterprise Institute called until recently "Religion, Philosophy and Public Policy." It was funded by some of this money also. Olin gave $90,520 in 2001 for the project.[21]

So What?

What does all of this mean? It's not illegal or immoral to seek money to pursue an agenda. Are the acoustics at Carnegie Hall distorted because Andrew Carnegie was a ruthless steel baron? Is Duke not a great university because it grew from tobacco riches?

What has been described here is not the same as the "monumental" use of riches to atone for rapacious economy activity. Some people with money — much of it with close ties to corporate agendas — began 30 years ago to use their funds to shape the political landscape to conform to their agendas.

These foundations did not put money into hard-edged religious advocacy groups to support evangelism. Peter Steinfels again:

> The world of religion is puzzling. Certain segments of it are distressingly adversarial. But (the culture-war types) did not have the standing, did not speak the language, did not know where the bodies were hidden — in short, could not carry out the same kind of campaign in the churches they were successfully waging in the political and university theaters. The emergence of a parallel "war of ideas" in the churches was slow to start....It has taken a while for the sponsors of the "war of ideas" to find their *condottieri* (hired guns) in the field of religion. The emergence of the Institute on Religion and Democracy is one of several indications that they have been found.[22]

Ask organizations about the source of their money and they get defensive, as George Weigel of the Ethics and Public Policy Center did in an interview eight years ago: "Why are you guys always looking for money problems?"[23]

Anyone who has worked or volunteered for a struggling non-profit knows the difficulty of staying afloat. Taking money from questionable sources can be tempting. Michael Lind, once executive editor of Irving Kristol's Olin-funded *National Interest,* warned in *Dissent* in Winter/ 1995:

> One by one every leading neoconservative publication or think tank over the past decade has come to depend on money from a few key foundations. Many were started in the first place by seed money from the foundations. Inevitably, this has promoted group think. This is not because of some centralized conspiracy imposing a party line.... The editors tend to censure themselves, for fear of appearing 'liberal' and losing that critical annual grant.[24]

Occasionally funders do retaliate. Richard Scaife took a grant away because the recipient strayed. Scaife spent money and energy in the 1990s trying to prove that Clinton friend and White House aide Vincent Foster was murdered. Two special prosecutors, including Kenneth Starr, ruled Foster's death a suicide.[25] Scaife abruptly ended his long history of generous grants to *The American Spectator* when it dared write that Foster committed suicide.

In the meantime, the money wave continues. Lots of organizations are surfing happily on its crest. It is important to know how this phenomenon has developed. And what is at stake.

Endnotes

[1] Reed "Contract with the American Family."
[2] Fineman 25.
[3] Martin 70.
[4] Foundation News.
[5] Howell *Funding the War on Ideas* 4.
[6] National Committee for Responsive Philanthropy 3.
[7] Phone interview.
[8] Phone interview.
[9] Dolny "What's In a Label?"
[10] Dolny "Think Tanks Y2K."

[11] Kaiser and Chinoy A1.

[12] Kaiser and Chinoy A1+.

[13] Miner; see National Committee for Responsive Philanthropy "Moving A Public Policy Agenda" for information about Olin and Bradley.

[14] Howell "Religion, Politics, Money and Power" 36.

[15] National Education Association.

[16] Steinfels 80-86.

[17] The $4.4 million figure was arrived at like this: The Media Transparency Project documented grants from conservative secular foundations of $3,579,000 between 1985 and 2001. Source: www.mediatransparency.org. About $479,500 arrived from December 1980 through January 1983 from the same foundations. Source: *Christianity and Crisis,* March 23 1983. Total: $4,058,500. That leaves 1983-1984 to be accounted for. (Assume an annual average as of $200,000.) That totals $4,458,000 from 1981 through 2001.

[18] Howell "LeFever at the Edge..." 35.

[19] Grant Data Project.

[20] Howell.

[21] Schedule of Grants 2001.

[22] Steinfels 85.

[23] Howell *Funding The War of Ideas.*

[24] Lind.

[25] Kaiser A2.

9
Aiming at General Conference 2004

General Conference 2004 is the focus of conservative renewal groups' strategies to remake The United Methodist Church. Their tactics are clear, their petitions are circulating and their recruiting is in high gear. The 2003 annual conferences where delegates will be selected is crucial.

Because General Conference is so central to United Methodist life and procedure, it is useful to review its purpose and shape.

General Conference is the only entity that speaks officially for the entire United Methodist Church. Policy flows from the General Conference, a body of United Methodists — half laity and half clergy — that gathers every four years. It occurs next in Pittsburgh, Pennsylvania, April 27-May 7, 2004.

The 994 delegates for 2004 will be elected by their peers through a formula that distributes the number by geographic conferences, nationally and internationally. They will spend two weeks debating and determining The United Methodist Church 's structure, laws and policies. About 2,500 guests and observers will encircle the official process.[1]

The United Methodist Church has its roots in the era when the United States was becoming a nation. As with the U.S. government, United Methodist Church processes include making policy by majority votes of elected representatives. It also has a structure of boards and agencies charged with enacting denominational policy.

Other things about General Conference:

- Bishops and the denomination's Judicial Council interpret its work in the intervening years.
- These gatherings become part of history. Within the denomination, it is common to refer to dynamics from, say, General Conference 1972 in Atlanta or 2000 in Cleveland.
- Men compose the majority of delegates, especially in the clergy ranks.
- General Conference delegates are predominantly white middle-aged to older adults.
- The conferences are filled with much of the same lobbying, maneuvering and favor-trading as secular political processes.
- Worship services and celebrations enliven the central policy-making function of General Conference.
- Efforts have been made — often led by the Council of Bishops — to draw attention away from the legislative activities with calls for a "kinder, gentler, more efficient" process. That would focus more on shared beliefs than on controversy — a movement that would have to buck history.
- General Conference ensures input from across the denomination, at best revealing many movements afoot in church and secular circles of U.S. society.
- With U.S. church membership declining and international membership increasing, the voice of delegates from outside the United States is expanding.
- Because of a new formula for selecting delegates, the Southeast and South Central regions of the United States and the international conferences will have more delegates, and the East, Midwest and West fewer, likely producing a more conservative voting tally at General Conference 2004.

Good News on the March

Good News led a training session on General Conference 2004 for United Methodists at the "Confessing the Faith" Conference in Indianapolis, Indiana, in October 2002. Good News petitions were ready. A representative of Good News had been on the road organizing for annual-conference delegate elections. Good News had been offered a $100,000 challenge grant for its General Conference fund.[2]

James V. Heidinger II, Good News president and chair of the Association for Church Renewal that convened the Indianapolis conference, reflected on previous General Conferences: The three in the 1980s were "devastating," but Cleveland 2000 — where Good News had a "war room" of 80 people — was terrific for their interests. Avoid complacency, he warned: "The other side will be back with great energy."

Scott Field, pastor of Wheatland-Salem United Methodist Church in Naperville, Illinois, and Good News director of legislative affairs, told the same meeting:

> We are the future of the church. The United Methodist Church is waking up and realizing its mission and purpose again.

Field said the Good News and Confessing Movement boards are working in coalition on delegate elections. Good News put its General Conference agenda into circulation early.[3] It has 51 points, which, if enacted, would produce a dramatically less prophetic church. Take five points:

- Push pastors to take reordination vows that meet Good News' doctrinal standard, jettisoning traditional freedom of the pulpit.
- Demand that all United Methodist seminary and university faculty "affirm classical theology."
- Dramatically curtail women's role in mission in The United Methodist Church.
- Make the mandatory apportionment system voluntary, undercutting the connectional church.
- Impose tight accountability rules — called for from an unaccountable body.

Good News board member Thomas Lambrecht told the Indianapolis meeting the petitions circulated there could be introduced at the annual conferences in 2003. "Basically one could just fill in the conference name," he said. Debating the petitions at annual conferences would be good training for General Conference, he said.

Joe Kilpatrick, a certified public accountant from Atlanta, gave a talk about how he had gotten elected to General Conference several times. A version appears in the March-April 2003 *Good News* magazine and on the *Good News* website. His direction:

- Pray for renewal.
- Learn the process.

- Be an aggressive Christian. He wrote campaign letters with lots of endorsements.
- Write a position paper.
- Join with other conservatives.
- Go early to annual conference.

Field challenged United Methodists at the Indianapolis conference: "We have a critically important task. We have to get as many delegates as possible to Pittsburgh."

Institute on Religion and Democracy

IRD has few troops to mobilize but works with Good News and others in the Association for Church Renewal to plan for moments like General Conference. And it's pushing its proposal to bury the General Board of Church and Society. (See Chapter 4.)

UM Action felt good about the 2000 General Conference and thanked supporters and the "entire growing renewal movement" for making its presence possible. It took some credit. Mark Tooley of the Institute for Religion and Democracy said:

> Thanks to UM Action and its supporters and friends, many key victories were won. All the glory goes to God, who is showing He still intends to use our church....UM Action for the last four years distributed our quarterly *UMAction Briefings* to hundreds of thousands of United Methodist homes. That made a big difference in informing and equipping the laity of our church.[4]

Now they and their conservative renewal colleagues are headed full steam for Pittsburgh.

Endnotes

[1] UMNS "How General Conference Works."

[2] Drawn from presentations by Field, Heidinger and Lambrecht "Confessing the Faith" Conference, 24-25 October 2002.

[3] http://wwwgoodnewsmag.org appearing 23 March 2003.

[4] *UMAction* "UM Action at General Conference" 5-6.

A Story
An Attempt at Informed Debate

The speech Bishop C. Joseph Sprague gave at Iliff School of Theology in Denver in January 2002 was intended to be provocative. He did not expect it to draw charges of heresy.

Sprague — of the Chicago Episcopal Area — has lived out his understanding of the Gospel in ways that have often challenged the church to grow. This is what he was about when he spoke at Iliff.

Drawing from "The Fully Human Jesus," chapter four of his then-forthcoming book, *Affirmations of a Dissenter,* Sprague confessed "candidly and vulnerably" who Jesus the risen Christ is for him. His intention was to encourage seekers — those engaged in such internal dialogues themselves.[1]

Much in the address was traditional: an affirmation of Jesus as fully divine and fully human, unique and normative. But Sprague also entered the realm of debate. The speech touched on several issues that Christian theologians have debated for millennia, including the power of symbol and myth, the nature of the virgin birth and resurrection of Jesus, the merit of various atonement theories, and the pluralistic nature of our world.

The first public response came some months later. Bishop Timothy W. Whitaker of the Florida Episcopal Area dissented from parts of what Sprague said and affirmed others. Whitaker emphasized his desire to engage Sprague in dialogue in a "joint commitment to pursue the truth."[2]

Six months after Sprague spoke at Iliff, conservative renewal groups within The United Methodist Church responded to the Iliff speech on their websites. Mark Tooley of the Institute on Religion and Democracy (IRD) wrote that the bishop had challenged various United Methodist articles of faith by publicly questioning "Jesus Christ's eternal deity, unique role as savior, virgin birth, physical resurrection, and atonement for the sins of the world."[3] His article was posted under the UM Action section of the IRD website.

Some critics suggested churches refuse to pay their share of the funds that support the national church, including bishops' salaries. By fall 2002, rumors began to circulate that formal charges would be filed against Sprague. Calls came for him to resign. He was accused of heresy.[4]

In an editorial in the November/December 2002 *Good News* magazine, James V. Heidinger II, president of Good News, accused Sprague of violating the vow he took when consecrated bishop to guard the faith, doctrine and discipline of the church against all that is contrary to God's word. Heidinger wrote:

> In every age, the church is threatened by those outside who
> would harm and destroy, and by those within who would ac-
> commodate the church to secular norms or harm the faithful
> by teaching false doctrine. Pastors can become predators
> and deceive their flock, causing great harm.

Bishop Marion Edwards of North Carolina and Bishop Michael Watson of South Georgia also voiced their dissent.[5] Bishop John McCleskey of South Carolina, on the other hand, said Sprague was engaging in the theological task urged of bishops by the *Book of Discipline*. He said Sprague should not resign, and affirmed dialogue and theological diversity. McCleskey said:

> We need each other's differing insights....It is time for us
> United Methodists to lay to rest theological perspectives
> which are focused on gaining, keeping, or reclaiming power
> and control — whether in the local congregation, the annual
> conference, or the general church.[6]

In response, IRD attacked both Sprague and McCleskey for promoting dialogue. IRD's response characterized Sprague as a heterodox, denying "nearly all of the Christian God's transcendent and personal qualities."[7]

Sprague continued to call for dialogue. He had written the book to provoke debate, not division. He said his call to ministry in The United Methodist Church was informed by the "conciliar nature of our polity...informed minds and warm hearts...hospitality and reason."[8]

Twenty-eight United Methodist clergy and laity filed a complaint against Sprague. They asked that he renounce publicly his contrary teaching or resign and surrender his ordination credentials.

When the complaint became public, Bishop Whitaker expressed dismay that the group had chosen the complaint process rather than engaging Sprague in dialogue. He told United Methodist News Service:

> I wrote a response to Bishop Sprague, and when I sent out the
> response I also sent a letter to members of the Council of Bish-
> ops. In the letter I rejected the suggestion that a complaint
> should be filed against Bishop Sprague.[9]

The supervisory process that follows a complaint is confidential, but before Sprague was aware charges had been filed, they appeared in the press. The supervisory response team that dealt with the charges ordered the complainants to apologize publicly.[10]

The supervisory team dropped the charges against Sprague, and, in an unusual move, decided to make the report of its process and ruling public. It did so because the procedure appeared in the press and because the "theological and doctrinal issues raised in the complaint are already a matter of considerable public debate within The United Methodist Church." Its recommendations:

• Sprague should clarify and reaffirm his adherence to the doctrinal standards of The United Methodist Church;
• The Council of Bishops should engage in theological reflection on issues of Christology, biblical authority and the mission of the church; and
• As many bishops and Sprague had requested from the beginning, he and those who filed charges against him should participate in a mediated, public dialogue.

After the dismissal, Sprague said, "It was my intent, in the Iliff lecture and with the book, to stimulate informed debate."[11]

He referred to Paragraph 104 in the *Book of Discipline:* Part of the theological task of United Methodists is "testing, renewal, elaboration, and application of our doctrinal perspective in carrying out our calling to spread scriptural holiness over the lands."[12]

Endnotes

[1] Sprague *Affirmations of a Dissenter* 36.

[2] Whitaker "A Response to Bishop Sprague" 6.

[3] Tooley "UM Bishop...."

[4] Rooney; Brown and Brown "Methodist Minister Rebels..."; Wildmon; Field, Regner "United Methodist Bishop..."; Sprague "I Can't Sit By..."; Heidinger "Are There Any..."; McMullen "Methodist Bishops..."; Heidinger "Good News Board"; Tooley "Florida Bishop...."

[5] Edwards "Reflections on Guarding..."; Regner "Bishop Edwards Becomes..."; Watson.

[6] McCleskey "Letter to Clergy of South Carolina Annual Conference."

[7] Regner "Heterodox Methodist Bishop...", IRD "Bishop McCleskey...."

[8] Sprague "I Can't Sit By...."

[9] Gilbert "Group Files Complaint...."

[10] Information on the complaint and ruling comes from: Gilbert "Complaints Dismissed...."

[11] Sprague "Dear Ones."

[12] Ibid.

Part 2
Who Will Decide?

Who Will Decide?
The Looming Battle
Over Doctrine
in The United Methodist Church

by The Rev. Scott Campbell

In September 2002, a group of theologians related to seven denominations in North America met in Dallas to draft a letter to *confessing Christians*. The letter sought to respond to questions, the most basic of which was why should confessing Christians remain in their churches?

The most substantive response was phrased as follows:

> ...the reason we cannot and must not leave our denomina-
> tions is that the Gospel can still be freely proclaimed in them
> and the sacraments administered without hindrance.

The letter was presented the following month to a group of Christians meeting at the "Confessing the Faith" Conference in Indianapolis, Indiana, a gathering of members of conservative renewal groups from the seven denominations. A significant portion of the conference was dedicated to working on a legislative agenda for the 2004 United Methodist General Conference. It is ironic that much of that work dealt with limiting the freedom of other Christians to freely proclaim the Gospel and administer the sacraments.

In the name of reclaiming doctrinal integrity, the conference advanced a number of petitions for General Conference, many designed to force others to conform to what the proponents call *classical Christianity.*

The Good News legislative agenda seeks to mandate fidelity on the part of clergy; faculty at United Methodist colleges, universities and seminaries; and board and agency personnel to an undefined set of theological propositions that comprise their concept of classical Christianity.

While not defined in the legislation, classical Christianity has been defined elsewhere in the writing of these groups as the doctrinal standards identified in *The Book of Discipline of The United Methodist Church.* These would likely include The Articles of Religion (Methodist), the Confession of Faith (Evangelical United Brethren) and the General Rules. John Wesley's sermons and explanatory notes on the New Testament also are often mentioned.

The problem is it is impossible to develop any single strand of doctrinal thinking that alone can be called classical. Methodism founder John Wesley himself was notoriously inconsistent about what he deemed to be essential to the faith.

From the earliest days of the Church, there have been matters around which Christians of good faith have seriously disagreed. One need not look beyond The Acts of the Apostles or the letters of Paul to discover that believers have never been of one opinion around a whole host of issues. Paul's quarrel with the Jerusalem Christians over whether Gentile converts needed to be circumcised was but one of the problems faced by the early church.

In nearly every instance, believers tended to separate into two distinct camps — those who held out for the purity of the tradition and those who sought to apply the principles of the tradition to shifting circumstances. Which of these strains shall we call classical Christianity?

Purity versus flexibility is an issue with which Jesus was acquainted. In Mark 2:27, he said to the purists of his day — the Pharisees: "The Sabbath was made for humankind and not humankind for the Sabbath!" Jesus knew the tension.

Wesley, too, weighed in on the matter. He had little patience with the idea that doctrine has ultimate — salvific — significance. In his sermon about those who build their houses on the sand, he said:

> Whereon do I build my expectation of entering into the kingdom of heaven? Is it not built on the sand? Upon my orthodoxy, or right opinions, which, by a gross abuse of

words, I have called faith? Upon my having a set of notions,
suppose(d) more rational or scriptural than others have?
Alas! what madness is this! Surely this is building on the
sand, or, rather, on the froth of the sea![1]

Role of doctrine

So what is the appropriate role for doctrine and for orthodoxy to play
in our church? How should The United Methodist Church define doctrinal integrity? What is normative for us?

The need for sound doctrine is not in dispute. The question is not
whether a church ought to articulate its theological beliefs, but, rather,
how such formulations ought to be used to *guide* the faithful.

Some churches are authoritarian in nature like the Roman Catholic
Church. The hierarchy of the church formulates and enforces church
law and doctrine. Some churches are traditionalist like the Orthodox
Church. Only what appears in the tradition of the church is permissible
in terms of liturgy or doctrine.

Still other churches are creedal, including the Lutheran and Anglican
churches. Orthodoxy is defined by conformity to a particular creedal
expression like the Augsburg or Westminster Confessions.

Until now, the Methodist family has chosen a different route from
many other Christians. With roots as a vital reform movement within a
classical tradition, we felt no need to form our own Methodist creeds.
Methodists have historically been far more concerned about living out
the Gospel in encounters with the world than we have been with developing and enforcing theological conformity.

Generations of Methodists have reached across significant theological disagreements to declare to one another Wesley's words: "If your
heart be as my heart, then give me your hand."

Wesley once summed up the doctrine of the Methodists in this way:

The fundamental doctrine of the people called Methodists is,
Whosoever will be saved, before all things it is necessary
that he hold the true faith — the faith which works by love;
which, by means of the love of God and our neighbour, produces both inward and outward holiness.[2]

Does this mean anything goes in the name of love? Not at all. The classical expressions of faith in the church universal and those adapted to

and adopted by our Methodist forebears serve as important correctives and guides to our common life.

Doctrine has primarily been understood as a tool to inform and guide the faithful. It has not been used as an instrument of inquisition. Our tradition is, by and large, one of openness, flexibility and breadth of spirit. We do not use doctrine as a club to coerce compliance, but as an indispensable aid in deepening our discipleship.

Wesley set the tone for this flexibility. He was a ruthless abridger and amender of the so-called classical doctrines. He took the 39 Articles of Religion of the Church of England, chopped off 15 and revised others to suit his own purposes. Albert Outler points out Wesley's penchant for borrowing notions that were appealing to him and incorporating them into his theology:

> The elements of his theology were adapted from many sources: The prime article of justification by faith from the reformers (Anglican) of the 16th century, the emphasis on the assurance of faith from the Moravian pietists; the ethical notions of divine-human synergism from the ancient Fathers of the Church, the idea of the Christian life as devotion from Taylor and others, the vision and program of "perfection" from Gregory of Nyssa.[3]

The General Conference of 1808 saw an end to this eclectic approach when the First Restrictive Rule was introduced to the Constitution, making further revisions of doctrine all but impossible. The result of that artificial freezing of one series of statements was that the Articles of Religion became less and less relevant to successive generations of Methodists. By the time the 20th century dawned, many in the pews viewed the Articles as relics of a distant past if they even knew of their existence.

Nevertheless, the Articles of Religion remain important guidelines for the church. But they must not be seen as the end of the road. They are guides along a journey.

Reinvigorating Doctrine

None of this addresses the far more important issue of how well Methodists have lived out what we say we believe. Proclamation of doctrine has been no guarantor that we would grasp what the Spirit was doing in our midst.

For instance, generations of Methodists perpetuated racist practices at the core of our polity, leading to schism in the church and, later, the creation of the Central Jurisdiction, a kind of Methodist apartheid system. It was with an awareness that our doctrine had failed to keep us from sin that the 2000 General Conference featured a service of repentance with sisters and brothers of historically Black Methodist churches. The service has been duplicated in conferences across the country.

The church has still to repent of the racism toward African-American sisters and brothers who stayed within the denomination.

We have had to understand in each age, with the guidance of the Holy Spirit, the specific applications of our doctrine. It is this impulse that led General Conference to include the following words in the doctrinal standards in the *Book of Discipline:*

> The United Methodist Church stands continually in need of
> doctrinal reinvigoration for the sake of authentic renewal,
> fruitful evangelism, and ecumenical dialogue. In this light,
> the recovery and updating of our distinctive doctrinal her-
> itage — catholic, evangelical, and reformed — is essential.[4]

This task calls for the repossession of our traditions as well as the promotion of theological inquiry both within the denomination and in our ecumenical efforts. All are invited to share in this endeavor to stimulate an active interest in doctrinal understanding in order to claim our legacy and to shape that legacy for the Church we aspire to be.

The center of Methodism has never been primarily doctrinal, but has always involved spreading the good news of God's gracious acts in Jesus Christ across the earth. This is in contrast to what we are seeing on the right, which is almost a deification of doctrine. William Sloane Coffin recently said:

> It is bad religion to deify doctrines and creeds. While indis-
> pensable to religious life, doctrines and creeds are only so as
> signposts. Love alone is the hitching post.[5]

The time has come to focus once more on the riches of our tradition. Let there be open debate about the meaning of the historic formulations of doctrine. The creation of doctrine is, after all, a human endeavor, undertaken in specific contexts throughout the long history of the church. The notion that the canon is closed on doctrine is a betrayal of our birthright.

Let there be broad inquiry into the articulations of our forebears in the faith, and let those expressions of the past continually be made new, incorporating the wisdom and insight of each generation. We must trust that what is of God will not pass away. It is the task of the church always to seek out the revealed Word of God in its own time and place. Rather than attempting to enforce lockstep, backward-looking conformity, the best that is in our tradition calls us to move forward boldly.

About the Author: The Rev. Scott Campbell is pastor at Harvard Epworth United Methodist Church in Cambridge, Massachusetts.

Endnotes

[1] Wesley "Upon Our Lord's Sermon on the Mount."
[2] Watson 34.
[3] Outler 119.
[4] The *Book of Discipline, 2000* ¶103 (59).
[5] Winkler.

Part 3
A Wake-Up Call

Study Guide:
An Invitation to Reflection
and Dialogue

by Scott Campbell and Bishop C. Dale White

For months, a skilled research team has searched the United Methodist archives, and studied documents and publications of conservative renewal movements related to The United Methodist Church. They have traced the history of these groups and the sources of their funding. The purpose has been to assure that United Methodists, along with those of other denominations, are fully informed on the goals, strategies and tactics of these groups.

The leaders of the conservative renewal groups operate with a narrowly focused theological and socio-political agenda. Many receive large grants from non-church organizations with a distinct political and ideological agenda unrelated to making disciples of Christ.

They are adamant that their vision of the theological foundations of the Church and its role in society is the whole truth. They make the bold assertion that they are the true standard bearers of the Wesleyan heritage and the only faithful guardians of evangelical Christianity.

There are many sincere, faithful Christians who count themselves as members and supporters of conservative renewal groups such as Good News, Renew, the Confessing Movement and related groups. This study's critique of these groups is in no way meant to question the integrity and faithfulness of these individuals. It is important, however, for them to be able to make informed decisions about what it is they are supporting.

Left unchallenged, the conservative renewal movements stand poised to dramatically change the character of our denomination. Is not this moment in history the time for the vast majority of committed United Methodists to awaken to what is happening in our beloved church?

It is said eternal vigilance is the price of freedom. Jesus warned the disciples they must not only be as harmless as doves, but wise as serpents (Matthew 10:16). Look carefully now at the contrast between the spirit and objectives of these groups and our United Methodist heritage as it is rooted firmly in Scripture.

Each of the following six sections highlights strategies and actions of conservative renewal groups and contrasts them with what have been traditional practices in The United Methodist Church. There are questions and Scripture for reflection and discussion in each section. The six sections are followed by "A Call to Action."

The material is suitable for personal reflection and small-group discussion, but the ultimate goal is to move people to act positively and creatively. It is imperative that concerned United Methodists act now.

Gather with others to build consensus on shared convictions and action strategies. Conservative renewal groups have learned that organization is the key to moving the church. Loyal United Methodists must now organize to help shape a future for The United Methodist Church that is consistent with its great heritage. The future of the church hangs in the balance.

1: Methods and Tactics

Observers of the conservative renewal groups often deplore their organizing tactics as unduly harsh and aggressive. A polarizing style of rhetoric foments divisiveness rather than dialogue and consensus. Inflammatory rhetoric sows fear rather than illumination.

Highly selective reporting is standard. Those writing for renewal publications often distort reality by focusing on snippets of events taken out of context. Participants in major church gatherings often come away inspired by uplifting music, excellent preachers, illuminating Bible study, only to be amazed at the hostile and misleading accounts printed in renewal literature like *Good News* magazine and the *UMAction* newsletter published by the Institute on Religion and

Democracy. How often is heard the response: "I cannot believe these people sat in the same meeting!"

From Our Tradition
John Wesley said, "...although a difference in opinions or modes of worship may prevent an entire external union, yet need it prevent our union in affection? Though we cannot think alike, may we not love alike? May we not be of one heart, though we are not of one opinion?"[1]

Reflection/Discussion Questions
1. Christians are called to "make disciples of all nations" (Matthew 28:16-20). A chronically quarreling, divided congregation or denomination is not an effective setting for outreach evangelism. How can we witness to the essentials of the Gospel without alienating others who may differ?
2. What needs to be done to make the church a sanctuary for thoughtful, respectful, vigorous debate on matters of faith, in a society where uncivil dogmatism seems to be increasing?
3. Some persons believe there are essentials of faith so vital as to justify defending them with hostile, inflammatory language and deceptive reporting. How do you respond to such a perspective?
4. How might the church relate to those who violate standards of thoughtful, compassionate dialogue on issues of faith?

From the Scriptures
Ephesians 4:35-5:2: "Put away from you all bitterness and wrath and anger and wrangling and slander, together with all malice, and be kind to one another, tenderhearted, forgiving one another, as God in Christ has forgiven you. Therefore be imitators of God, as beloved children, and live in love, as Christ loved us and gave himself up for us, a fragrant offering and sacrifice to God."

2. Prophetic Ministry
The actions of the conservative renewal movements weaken and discredit the prophetic ministry of the church. Their targeting of the United Methodist General Board of Church and Society, United Methodist Women and the Women's Division of the United Methodist General Board of Global Ministries is an attempt to eliminate organizations

and agencies most clearly charged by the *Discipline* to lead the church in study, witness and action on policies of peace and justice. Have they forgotten John Wesley's declaration that he "knows of no religion but social, no holiness but social holiness."[2]

An illustration: With the United States' increased emphasis on military solutions to international problems, these groups are quick to cry "un-American" as Christians witness for peace. Following the Sept. 11, 2001, attack, the Women's Division published a statement urging President Bush to use diplomatic means, not war, to bring the terrorists to justice. The division made a commitment through prayer, study and action to continue the search for peace with justice.

The president of Good News was quick to add the charge "virulently anti-American!" to the familiar polemic against the "radical feminist, pro-abortion, anti-evangelical, anti-free market, pro-homosexual attitude exhibited by the Women's Division New York leadership and materials."[3]

From Our Tradition:

Speaking about war, John Wesley said, "There is a still more horrid reproach to the Christian name, yea, to the name of man, to all reason and humanity. There is war in the world! War between men! War between Christians! I mean between those that bear the name of Christ and profess to walk as he taught us to walk. Now who can reconcile War, I will not say to Religion, but to any degree of reason or common sense? What an amazing way of deciding controversies."[4]

The United Methodist Book of Resolutions addresses war: "We deplore war and urge the peaceful settlement of all disputes among nations. From the beginning, the Christian conscience has struggled with the harsh realities of violence and war, for these evils clearly frustrate God's loving purposes for humankind. Some of us believe that war, and other acts of violence, are never acceptable to Christians. We also acknowledge that most Christians regretfully realize that, when peaceful alternatives have failed, the force of arms may be preferable to unchecked aggression, tyranny and genocide."[5]

Reflection/Discussion Questions

1. Is it unpatriotic to witness for peace in a time of war? Is the traditional Methodist position that "war is incompatible with the teach-

ings and example of Christ" no longer realistic? Is the just-war doctrine still useful after its systematic violation in all of the wars of the past century?

2. How can our sanctuaries be oases of just peacemaking in our families, our local neighborhoods, our nation and our global community?
3. As we continue to be faithful in relief and development ministries to alleviate hunger and poverty, how can we exercise our political ministry to advocate for economic justice? Do you know about the work of Bread for the World, the foremost Christian advocacy group for policies to alleviate hunger? Check out www.bread.org.
4. How do you see yourself as a follower of the Prince of Peace?

From the Scriptures
Micah 4:3: "He shall judge between many people, and shall arbitrate between strong nations far away; they shall beat their swords into plowshares, and their spears into pruning hooks; nation shall not lift up sword against nation, neither shall they learn war any more."

Matthew 5:9: "Blessed are the peacemakers, for they will be called children of God."

3. Attacks on Women

Read again the section describing the attacks on United Methodist Women and the Women's Division in Chapter 4. Discuss the paragraphs under the subheading "In Sum, Be Alert." The study concludes that the announced strategies to reform the Women's Division are meant to weaken it. They would remove women from their historic leadership in the denomination's mission program, and would silence significantly women's voices within the denomination's decision-making arenas. This is a movement fully in keeping with conservative, fundamentalist thinking that requires women to be subservient to men. This runs counter to the function given the Women's Division in *The Book of Discipline:*

> The Women's Division shall be actively engaged in fulfilling the mission of Christ and the Church and shall interpret the purpose of United Methodist Women. With continuing awareness of the concerns and responsibilities of the Church in today's world, the Women's Division shall be an advocate for

the oppressed and dispossessed with special attention to the needs of women and children; shall work to build a supportive community among women; and shall engage in activities that foster growth in the Christian faith, mission education, and Christian social involvement throughout the organization.[6]

From Our Tradition

John Wesley saw "women were persons in Christ equally with men." Writing to a Mrs. Bennis in January 1774, he said:

A will steadily and uniformly devoted to God is essential to a state of sanctification, but not an uniformity of joy or peace or happy communion with God. These may rise and fall in various degrees; nay, and may be affected either by the body or by diabolical agency, in a manner which all our wisdom can neither understand nor prevent....You are not sent to Waterford to be useless. Stir up the gift of God which is in you; gather together those that have been scattered abroad, and make up a band, if not a class or two. Your best way would be to visit from house to house. By this means you can judge of their conduct and dispositions in domestic life, and may have opportunity to speak to the young of the family. By motion you will contract warmth; by imparting life you will increase yourself.

Reflection/Discussion Questions

1. Do you believe the above mandate given to the Women's Division is consistent with the Great Commission: "Go therefore and make disciples of all nations" (Matthew 28:19)? Would you rewrite the *Discipline* paragraph on the Women's Division? How?
2. Remembering that more than half of all United Methodists are women, how can we assure that their voices are heard, their gifts received, their spiritual journeys enriched, in full partnership with men?
3. Since a major share of all mission giving in United Methodism comes through the activities of women, is it appropriate that United Methodist Women has a strong voice in assuring that the resources go to enrich the lives of women, children and youth around the world?
4. What do you believe is the purpose and motivation behind continuing attacks on the Women's Division?

From the Scriptures
Romans 12:6-9: "We have gifts that differ according to the grace given to us: prophecy, in proportion to faith; ministry, in ministering; the teacher, in teaching; the exhorter, in exhortation; the giver, in generosity; the leader, in diligence; the compassionate, in cheerfulness. Let love be genuine; hate what is evil, hold fast to what is good; love one another with mutual affection; outdo one another in showing honor."

4. Issues of Power

The following is an excerpt from a new book by Thomas C. Oden, a theologian who sits on the boards of directors of the Institute for Religion and Democracy, the Confessing Movement, and Lifewatch:

> Religious institutions, publishing houses, mission boards and seminaries have been seized in an unfriendly takeover by liberal church leadership....There is little hint of recognition among those who have stolen the institutions that they are the least bit culpable. They shamelessly imagine themselves to be heroes — even heroes of faith.
>
> Among the most insidious offenders are the liturgical experimenters, the sexual liberators, and the doctrinal revisionists who occupy lecterns and pulpits yet remain functional agnostics and deliberate agents of secular liberation. It will not be easy to tell these unfaithful ones the truth or to break through their self-deception. But this is precisely the task that faces the faithful today. Little will change until *charges are stated clearly and evidence is presented in fair hearings.*[7] (Emphasis added.)

Oden is advocating a strategy for seizing power in the church. It is a plan that calls for filing charges against those with whom he disagrees. Elsewhere he calls for lawsuits in the civil courts to remove the property of congregations he judges to be unfaithful to orthodoxy.[8] His language is filled with disparaging and demeaning characterizations of those he deems to be his opponents.

From Our Tradition
"If thine heart is as my heart, if thou lovest God and all mankind, I ask no more: Give me thine hand."[9]

Reflection/Discussion Questions

1. Some within The United Methodist Church have become increasingly litigious in the last decade, reflecting trends in the broader society. What do you think about this tendency? How should Christians resolve their disputes? Read Matthew 18:15-20.
2. Do you believe the traditional structures for establishing policy in The United Methodist Church — conferencing together, electing representatives to General Conference, and electing members to the governing bodies of boards and agencies are adequate to express the will of the church?
3. What are the limits to seeking power in the church? What power issues are raised by the growth of the conservative renewal movements? How is power handled in your local church? Can you suggest some guidelines for the Christian use of power?

From the Scriptures

I Corinthians 6:1-7a: "When any of you has a grievance against another, do you dare to take it to court before the unrighteous, instead of taking it before the saints?...I say this to your shame. Can it be that there is no one among you wise enough to decide between one believer and another, but a believer goes to court against a believer — and before unbelievers at that? In fact, to have lawsuits at all with one another is already a defeat for you."

5. Issues of Doctrine

James V. Heidinger II, president of Good News and editor of *Good News* magazine, writing in the aftermath of gains made by conservative renewal groups at the 2000 General Conference, announced in an exuberant editorial that the battle over homosexuality had ended. It had been won by the conservatives. The next frontier, he declared, was doctrine.[10]

True to his word, Good News has prepared a legislative onslaught for the 2004 General Conference. The main thrust of a series of petitions is the requirement that clergy, seminary professors, and board and agency personnel be required to proclaim solely those theological concepts deemed by the conservative renewal groups to be within the bounds of *classical Christianity*. Expulsion from the church — or firing in the case of board and agency staff — is possible for those who fail to comply. The proposed legislation calls upon bishops to enforce these standards or face trial.

While the would-be laws do not explicitly declare which doctrines are considered classical, the proponents have elsewhere indicated they intend these to include a belief in the physical resurrection of Christ, the virgin birth and a particular understanding of the atonement.

While there are many in the church who would have little difficulty affirming such articulations of Christian doctrine, there are others who would not be so quick to attach themselves to one way of understanding these concepts.

Such persons understand one task of theology to be the exploration of historical formulations of the faith in order to mine their deeper meaning. They seek continually to make such ideas relevant to a post-enlightenment world. They push against the limits of the words we use to tell our faith stories to find new vitality in old doctrine.

Such exploration could become an ecclesial crime under the proposed legislation. Conducting local-church study groups that consider alternative meanings to ancient interpretations of Scripture could become grounds for defrocking clergy. Who will decide where the new limits will be placed? Is this how we want to spend the time, money and energy of the church over the next decades, while the world goes unconvinced of the power of the Gospel we proclaim?

From Our Tradition
John Wesley is often cited in such debates. He embraced an earlier statement of Richard Baxter"s: "In necessary things, unity; in disputed (some have *doubtful)* things, liberty; in all things, charity."

The more common version of this quotation is: "In things essential unity, in non-essentials diversity, and in all things charity."

At first glance, this would seem to provide a specific path on doctrine for United Methodists. The only trouble is that Wesley's list of essentials shifted continually throughout his life. It is an impossible task to cull a definitive list from his writings. The one constant in all of his formulations of things essential, however, seems to be the requirement that the believer have a heart given over to the love of God and neighbor.[11]

Reflection/Discussion Questions
1. What do you consider essential beliefs for a Christian? For a United Methodist? Is there room in the church for disagreement and debate?

Would you seek to impose your views on everyone else?
2. Over the years, many persons have been drawn to The United Methodist Church because of its spirit of openness, its willingness to "think and let think." What place does this open spirit play in your life as a United Methodist? Is it important to you? Why or why not?
3. Jesus often rebuked the Pharisees and Scribes for their elevation of doctrine above compassion, for observance of the law ahead of love for persons. Are we running the risk of reforming The United Methodist Church in the image of the Pharisees?
4. What do you see as the most important issues on which to expend our church's resources for the next 10 years?

From the Scriptures
I Corinthians 13:1-2: "If I speak in the tongues of mortals and of angels, but do not have love, I am a noisy gong or a clanging cymbal. And if I have prophetic powers, and understand all mysteries and all knowledge, and if I have all faith, so as to remove mountains, but do not have love, I am nothing."

6. Issues of Accountability

There has been much talk in recent years about the need to hold others accountable in The United Methodist Church. The Coalition for United Methodist Accountability was organized by the conservative renewal movements for just such a purpose. Its self-declared mandate has been to hold leaders in The United Methodist Church accountable to the *Discipline* of the church, and where such persons are deemed to be in breach of the rules, to seek to bring charges against them. Clergy have been brought to trial for blessing unions among same-sex couples, and bishops have been charged for not prosecuting such offenders vigorously enough. Most recently, Bishop C. Joseph Sprague has been charged with heresy for expressing his views in a manner not seen as sufficiently orthodox by some. All of this has taken place in the name of greater accountability.

One problem with this focus on accountability is that it is selective. Although The United Methodist Church has often decried militarism, no pastor has yet been charged with unfaithfulness for praying over a nuclear submarine that holds within it the power to obliterate large segments of the planet.[12]

Nor has any pastor been charged with disobeying the order and discipline of The United Methodist Church for supporting the war against Iraq, despite the fact that our *Book of Discipline* declares war to be a practice incompatible with the teachings of Christ.[13] No one has been brought up on charges for supporting capital punishment, although our General Conference has declared the church to be against it.

This said, it is not the opinion of those producing this study that such offenses should be prosecuted in church trials. Such uses of this means of last resort would be utterly inappropriate.

From Our Tradition

United Methodists have long believed that accountability is not about seeking to penalize those with whom we disagree, but is about being in covenant with one another, about watching over each other in love. The Wesleyan class meeting that was so instrumental in forming early Methodism understood accountability to be a matter of praying for and with one another, of seeking to do good together and refraining from doing harm, and of joining with one another in disciplined spiritual practices.

We support such an understanding of covenant in the contemporary church. Rather than seeking to develop more ways to seek retribution against one another, we call upon the General Conference to find ways to build restorative models into the accountability structures of the church.

1. Paragraph 2702 in the *Book of Discipline* lists a number of offenses for which clergy can be tried. Sexual misconduct, crime and child abuse are listed. It is clear that the church must hold its leaders accountable for observing responsible standards of behavior. There are other items in the list that are of a different nature — disobedience to the order and discipline of the church, behavior declared by the General Conference to be incompatible with Christian teaching, and disseminating doctrine contrary to the established standards of The United Methodist Church. Should these sorts of offenses be dealt with in the same way as the other offenses? Why or why not?
2. What does it mean to watch over one another in love?
3. What is the source of Christian accountability?
4. Bishop Peter Storey of South Africa once commented that when he

went into conflicted churches, he would hold up a Bible and a book of discipline. He would tell the congregations they could use either book to solve their difficulties. He was dismayed that churches almost always chose the book of discipline. He said people preferred winners and losers rather than new relationships. Which book would you choose?

From the Scriptures
Ephesians 4:1-3: "I therefore, the prisoner in the Lord, beg you to lead a life worthy of the calling to which you have been called, with all humility and gentleness, with patience, bearing with one another in love, making every effort to maintain the unity of the Spirit in the bond of peace."

A Call to Action

Concerned about what you have read in this book? Then it's time to take action. Help to shape the future of United Methodism. Hearts need to be opened and minds need to be changed if we are to maintain what we love about The United Methodist Church and become the church God calls us to be. Here are ways you can make a positive difference.

▶ Pray daily for The United Methodist Church, its people and its minisry. Pray that the open spirit that has drawn so many to our church through the years will not be lost.

▶ Convene a study group in your local church to read and discuss this book. Obtain literature from the conservative renewal groups if you have not seen it before. Visit their web pages. Then decide for yourselves if the church that conservative renewal groups seek is the church you want.

▶ Give a copy of this book to your pastor, lay leader and others in your local church. Ask them to read it, and tell them you'd like to discuss it with them.

▶ Write a review of this book for your church newsletter. Make copies available so others can read it.

▶ Contact the delegates to General and Jurisdictional Conference from your annual conference to urge them to read this book. A list of delegates is available at your annual conference headquarters and should be available online http://umc.org/gc 2004/ by mid- to late-summer 2003. Tell the delegates you will be contacting them in a few weeks to discuss with them issues raised in the book.

▶ Write a letter to your bishop asking whether she or he has received and read a copy of this book. If not, offer to provide a copy.

▶ If you are reading this book before 2003 annual conference sessions, let it inform you input and decisions about those you or the annual-conference members from your church will elect as General Conference delegates.

▶ Find out more about the work being done by national United Methodist agencies. Support this work when you believe it is a faithful expression of the Christian faith. Give constructive input about how you think it can be more effective. Contacts include:
  • General Board of Church and Society: http://www.umc-gbcs.org/.
  • General Board of Global Ministries: http://gbgm-umc.org/.
  • Women's Division of the General Board of Global Ministries: http://gbgm-umc.org/Womens-Division/.
  • General Commission on the Status and Role of Women: http://gcsrw.org/.
  • General Commission on Religion and Race: http://www.gcrr.org/.

▶ Join with others who are committed to monitoring what the conservative renewal movement is doing. One such group is the Methodist Federation for Social Action — www.mfsaweb.org. There may be others as well. Seek out people who share your concerns and work together to make sure that accurate information is available within your local church, district and annual conference.

▶ Write a letter to your annual conference newspaper and district newsletter commending this book to others and urging them to acquire a copy.

▶ When you see church publications using wedge issues to divide the church, contact the editors and tell them that you do not appreciate what they are doing to our church. It is not problematic to discuss difficult issues, and even to be passionate. It is problematic when advocates of a certain perspective provide misleading information and caricature those with different opinions.

▶ Write letters to publications like *Good News* and *UMAction* challenging them to change the way they sensationalize news coverage and analysis.

► Contact people who are providing positive, constructive leadership in the church and encourage them to keep up the good work.

► Make a contribution to help defray the cost of publishing and distributing this book. Checks can be made out to: Hennepin Avenue UMC CIPUM and sent to Peter Barnett, Hennepin Avenue United Methodist Church, 511 Groveland Ave., Minneapolis, MN 55403.

► Finally, in all of your dealings with others in the church, maintain a civil, respectful and open attitude. As Mahatma Gandhi once said, "We must be the change that we wish to see."

Endnotes

[1] Wesley "Catholic Spirit."

[2] Wesley preface to *Sacred Hymns and Poems.*

[3] Heidinger "Time for a Change...."

[4] Wesley "Doctrine on Original Sin."

[5] From the Social Principles, *Book of Resolutions 2000.*

[6] *The Book of Discipline, 2000* ¶1317.

[7] Oden "How Orthodoxy is Renewing United Methodism" 26.

[8] Oden "The Trust Clause Governing Use of Property in The United Methodist Church" http://www.goodnewsmag.org/news/122902TrustClause_FULL.htm as appearing 23 March 2003.

[9] Wesley "Catholic Spirit."

[10] Heidinger editorial from *Good News* July-August 2000.

[11] Mead.

[12] *Book of Resolutions 2000,* Resolutions 306-318.

[13] *The Book of Discipline, 2000* ¶165 C.

Glossary

Aldersgate Renewal Ministries: Founded in 1977 as the United Methodist Renewal Services Fellowship, Inc. Describes itself as a "network of United Methodists who are praying and working together for the spiritual renewal of The United Methodist Church, by the power of the Holy Spirit." Sponsors Aldersgate, an annual conference on the Holy Spirit.

Alliance for Marriage: Promotes marriage and addresses the issue of fatherless families in the United States. Favors the federal marriage constitutional amendment, which would limit the definition of marriage to the union of a man and a woman.

American Anglican Council: A conservative renewal movement within the Episcopal Church that seeks to "affirm biblical authority and Anglican orthodoxy" and is oriented toward traditional forms of evangelism.

American Enterprise Institute for Public Policy Research: A Washington, D.C.-based non-profit research organization founded in 1943 whose research agenda supports "limited government, private enterprise, vital cultural and political institutions, and a strong foreign policy and national defense."

American Family Association: A renewal association dedicated to upholding "traditional family values," targeting primarily the influence of media on society (e.g., the entertainment industry's "glorification" of pre-marital sex, pornography, television shows with gay characters). Founded in 1977 by United Methodist ordained minister, Donald Wildmon, as the National Federation for Decency.

Annual conference: The basic organizational body in The United Methodist Church. Includes all United Methodist churches within a geographically defined area. Annual conferences in the United States are grouped into five geographic jurisdictions. Lay and clergy members of annual conferences elect delegates to general and jurisdictional conferences. Annual conference members are responsible for the program and administration of the work of the annual conference and its local churches. Annual conference membership consists of an equal number of lay and clergy members. At least one layperson from each pastoral charge is to be a member. (From *A Dictionary for United Methodists,* by Alan K. Waltz, Copyright ©1991 by Abingdon Press.)

Asbury College: Located in Wilmore, Kentucky. Founded in 1890 as Kentucky Holiness College. Renamed to honor Francis Asbury. Describes itself as "evangelical in its religious commitment and bound by its bylaws to those doctrinal standards established by John Wesley and his immediate successors." Not supported financially by The United Methodist Church.

Asbury Theological Seminary: Founded in 1923 "to prepare and send forth a well-trained, sanctified, Spirit-filled, evangelistic ministry to spread scriptural holiness around the world." Conservative renewal groups have many ties to the school in the form of faculty and supporters. Has become a center of renewal theology. Original campus in Wilmore, Kentucky. Additional campus in Orlando, Florida. Not an official United Methodist seminary.

Association for Church Renewal (ACR): Founded in 1996. An association of executives and leaders of church renewal organizations and ministries related to mainline denominations in the United States and Canada. Members include the American Anglican Council, Good News, Renew, the Institute on Religion and Democracy, Presbyterian Layman, the Confessing Movement (UMC), Transforming Congregations (UMC), and Bristol House, Ltd. James Heidinger II, president of Good News, chairs the association.

The Book of Discipline: *"The Book of Discipline* is the book of law of The United Methodist Church. *The Discipline* is the instrument for setting forth the laws, plan, polity, and process by which United Methodists govern themselves." (From *The Book of Discipline of The United Methodist Church, 2000.)* Changes to *The Book of Discipline* are made at General Conference sessions held every four years.

Bristol Bible Curriculum: An education curriculum "theologically focused on Methodist-Wesleyan doctrine" and "based on a high view of the Scriptures, pointing students to a personal relationship with Jesus Christ."

Central conferences: Organizational structures established for the work of The United Methodist Church in countries other than the United States of America. The number and boundaries are determined by the General Conference. Each central conference oversees the work of annual conferences, provisional annual conferences and mission conferences within its boundaries. Functions in much the same way as jurisdictional conferences in the United States. (From *A Dictionary for United Methodists,* by Alan K. Waltz, Copyright ©1991 by Abingdon Press.)

Coalition for United Methodist Accountability (CUMA): Established in 2000 by representatives of Good News, the Institute on Religion and Democracy, and the Confessing Movement. A February 16, 2000, press release says the coalition has assembled "a team of eminent attorneys and legal advisors who will be prepared to respond to ensure accountability in the order and administration of the church." Has supported the filing of charges against several church leaders, including bishops, where a conviction can mean a suspension or removal from the ordained ministry.

Confessing Movement: Emerged in The United Methodist Church in 1994-95 and claims to introduce a renewed theological focus to the church with an emphasis on encouraging laity and clergy to explicity "confess the person, work, and reign of Jesus Christ." This movement is dedicated to reforming the denomination rather than leaving it.

Confessing theologians: A group of theologians from seven denominations who convened in September 2002 under the leadership of United Methodist renewal leader and Institute on Religion and Democracy Chair Thomas C. Oden. Produced "Be Steadfast: A Letter to Confessing Christians," in which they urged confessing-movement members to stay in their denominations.

Conservative renewal movements: Refers to the various groups, including Good News, UM Action, the Confessing Movement, and the Institute on Religion and Democracy, among others, that are proponents of reforming their denominations to reflect a "more evangelical/orthodox faith" as seen in the traditional church creeds. Advocates of "the primacy of Scripture." Opposed to "theological pluralism." Concerned with church doctrine and social and moral issues.

Course of Study: The Course of Study for Ordained Ministry established by the Board of Higher Education and Ministry of The United Methodist Church as an alternate educational route for people seeking to serve as pastors in

United Methodist congregations, but who cannot commit to full- or part-time formal seminary training because of time, career or funding constraints. Participants receive theological education on weekends or during the summer at seminaries.

Ethics and Public Policy Center: Established in 1976 to "clarify and reinforce the bond between the Judeo-Christian moral tradition and the public debate over domestic and foreign-policy issues." Promotes Western ethical ideals and uses "religiously-based moral values" to analyze current issues. Examines the public-policy positions of various religions.

Focus on the Family: Founded in 1977 by James C. Dobson. Has grown from a book on child discipline and a 25-minute weekly broadcast to include a wide array of programs, projects and ministries, including broadcast programs, online programs, publications and resource production.

A Foundation for Theological Education (AFTE): Founded by Edmund W. Robb Jr. in 1977 to provide scholarships for evangelical students working on doctorates in theological areas. John Wesley Fellows teach at numerous United Methodist and other seminaries. Produces *Catalyst,* a quarterly newsletter for United Methodist seminarians, which promotes classical and evangelical Christianity.

General Board of Church and Society of The United Methodist Church (GBCS): One of four international general program boards of The United Methodist Church. Based in Washington, D.C. in the United Methodist Building across from the U.S. Capitol. Purpose is to seek the implementation of the Social Principles of The United Methodist Church (as stated in *The Discipline)* and other policy statements of the General Conference on Christian social concerns.

General Board of Global Ministries of The United Methodist Church (GBGM): One of four international general program boards of The United Methodist Church. Based in New York City. The mission agency of The United Methodist Church. The official goals: Witness to the Gospel for initial decision to follow Jesus Christ; strengthen, develop and renew Christian congregations and communities; alleviate human suffering — help initiate, strengthen and support the spiritual, physical, emotional and social needs of people; and seek justice, freedom and peace. The Women's Division is one unit of the board.

General Commission on Religion and Race (GCORR): Founded in 1968. General agency of The United Methodist Church. Promotes ethnic and racial inclusiveness in the total life and mission of the church.

General Commission on the Status and Role of Women (GCSRW): Founded in 1968. A general agency of The United Methodist Church. Charged with working to achieve the full and equal participation and responsibility of women in the church.

General Conference: Highest legislative body in the denomination. Meets in the spring every four years. The next meeting is April 27-May 7, 2004, in Pittsburgh, Pennsylvania. Composed of an equal number of lay and clergy delegates elected by their annual conferences. Primary responsibility to enact legislation that establishes the conditions for membership, defines the powers and duties of the clergy, defines the powers and duties of the conferences, establishes the powers and duties of the bishops, provides for a judicial system within the church, establishes the budget for the denomination, and establishes legislation governing the work of the local church and general agencies. (From *A Dictionary for United Methodists,* by Alan K. Waltz, Copyright ©1991 by Abingdon Press.)

Good News/*Good News:* A renewal movement and magazine created by Charles Keysor in 1967 to promote representation of those with more evangelical or traditional views in the church. Created as A Forum for Scriptural Christianity. Headquartered in Wilmore, Kentucky. James Heidinger II is president of Good News and publisher of *Good News* magazine. Keeping with one of its goals to "create and/or assist in creating supplemental church structures if necessary," oversees Renew Women's Network, the movement challenging the program of the Women's Division and United Methodist Women. Has been a force behind many of the renewal groups within The United Methodist Church.

Great Commission: Based on Matthew 28:19-20: "Go therefore and make disciples of all nations, baptizing them in the name of the Father and of the Son and of the Holy Spirit, and teaching them to obey everything that I have commanded you. And remember, I am with you always, to the end of the age" (New Revised Standard Version). Christians have various interpretations on how to fulfill the Great Commission ranging from explicit witnessing to administering a health clinic for the homeless.

The Institute on Religion and Democracy (IRD): Ecumenical think tank that seeks to renew the church under the tenets of the conservative renewal agenda. Publishes *Faith and Freedom, UMAction, Episcopal Action* and *Presbyterian Action.* Former United Methodist and now Epicopalian Diane Knippers is president. United Methodist theologian Thomas C. Oden is the chair.

Institute on Religion and Public Life: An interreligious, nonpartisan research and education institute that's purpose is to advance a religiously informed public philosophy for the ordering of society. Publishes the journal *First Things,* edited by Richard John Neuhaus.

Judicial Council: Highest judicial body or *court* of The United Methodist Church. Comprised of nine members elected by the General Conference and guided by *The Book of Discipline.* Determines the constitutionality of acts or proposed acts of the General, jurisdictional, central and annual conferences or other official bodies of The United Methodist Church.

Jurisdictional conference: United Methodist annual conferences in the United States are grouped into five geographic jurisdictions: North Central, Northeastern, South Central, Southeastern, Western. Jurisdictional conferences are responsible for election of bishops.

Lifewatch: Founded by nine pastors and laypeople meeting in Washington, D.C. in August 1987 under the original name of Taskforce of United Methodists on Abortion and Sexuality (TUMAS). Critical of the church's position on abortion. Champions anti-abortion petitions at General Conference.

Methodist Federation for Social Action (MFSA): Independent organization of United Methodists. Supports and augments peace-and-justice ministries at the local, conference and national levels of the church. Has 38 chapters. Areas of focus include racial justice, economic justice, inclusiveness, empowerment of women, peace and disarmament, a just peace in the Middle East, and environmental justice. Founded in 1907 as the Methodist Federation for Social Service to direct church attention to the human suffering among the working class. Spearheaded drive for the denomination's first social creed in 1908.

Missiologist: An individual who studies the mission of the church, including concepts and theology of mission.

The Mission Society for United Methodists: Formed in 1984 as an alternative missionary-sending agency to The United Methodist Church's General Board of Global Ministries in response to some clergy and laity's disagreement with the theology, policy and program of the board's mission program.

National Council of Churches (NCC): Principal ecumenical agency of Christians in the United States. Founded in 1950. Headquartered in New York City. Includes 36 denominations from Protestant, Anglican and Orthodox churches, including The United Methodist Church. Works on a variety of issues, including peace and justice, poverty, family ministries, and interfaith dialogue. Provided for the translation process that produced the New Revised Standard Version of the Bible. Sponsors humanitarian work in more than 80 countries through Church World Service. Representatives of member churches convene annually at the council's General Assembly.

Neoconservative: Generally liberals, or in the case of Irving Kristol and his allies in New York City, Marxists, who opposed the Vietnam War, but became hawks on international matters while remaining close to the labor movement and leary of the domestic social agenda of the political right. Names associated with neoconservatives include William Kristol, Irving's son; Jeane Kirkpatrick; the late Daniel Patrick Moynihan; the late Henry "Scoop" Jackson; Norman Podhoretz, especially when he edited *Commentary* magazine; Midge Dechter; Michael Novak; Richard John Neuhaus. The name was applied to them about 30 years ago by socialist Michael Harrington.

Presybterian Lay Committee: A conservative renewal group within the Presbyterian Church (USA). Advocates emphasis on biblical infallibility and Jesus as the only path to salvation. Founded in 1965. Publisher of the *Presbyterian Layman.*

Re-Imagining Conference: The 1993 Re-Imagining Conference was organized by an ecumenical group of volunteer clergy and laity to respond to the goals of the World Council of Churches' Ecumenical Decade: Churches in Solidarity with Women. Held in Minneapolis, Minnesota. Drew more than 2,000 people from around the world seeking to increase inclusiveness toward women in the church. Was attacked by conservative renewal groups such as Good News and the Presbyterian Lay Committee.

Religious Coalition on Reproductive Choice: A coalition of national organizations from 15 denominations, movements and faith groups including The United Methodist Church, the Episcopal Church, the Presbyterian Church (USA), the United Church of Christ, and the Conservative and Reform movements of Judaism. Dedicated to preserving reproductive choice as an element of religious liberty. Founded in 1973 as the Religious Coalition for Abortion Rights in response to efforts to overturn Roe versus Wade.

Renew Women's Network: Under the umbrella of Good News. Geared toward supporting evangelical, orthodox women within The United Methodist Church. Has spearheaded General Conference efforts to weaken the Women's Division and make United Methodist Women optional in the local church. Headed by Faye Short. Based in Cornelia, Georgia.

Schools of Christian Mission: A program of mission-education including three studies a year — spiritual-growth, geographic and social-justice issue. Sponsored by United Methodist Women and, in some annual conferences, by other groups within the conference, especially annual conference boards of global ministries. Open to everyone concerned about mission. Held across the United States annually.

Taskforce of United Methodists on Abortion and Sex (TUMAS): See Lifewatch.

Transforming Congregations: A network of United Methodist congregations. Promotes the belief that homosexual practice is a sin. Seeks to transform homosexuals into living a heterosexual lifestyle.

UM Action/*UMAction:*** A program and quarterly publication, headed by Mark Tooley of the Institute on Religion and Democracy. "Working for Scripture-based reform" in the United Methodist denomination.

United Methodist Women (UMW): A local-church membership organization for women. Women's Division of the General Board of Global Ministries is the parent organization. Purpose: "The organized unit of United Methodist Women shall be a community of women whose Purpose is to know God and to experience freedom as whole persons through Jesus Christ; to develop a creative, supportive fellowship; and to expand concepts of mission through participation in the global ministries of the Church" *(The Book of Discipline, 2000).* Every local church shall have an organized unit of the United Methodist Women. Funds raised by units support mission locally, nationally and internationally. Close to 1 million members.

Women's Division of the General Board of Global Ministries: A unit of the United Methodist General Board of Global Ministries. Actively engaged in fulfilling the mission of Christ and the church. Interprets the Purpose of United Methodist Women. Advocates for the oppressed and dispossessed with special attention to the needs of women, children and youth. Works to build a supportive community among women. Helps foster growth in the Christian faith, mission education and Christian social involvement (from *The Book of Discipline*).

World Council of Churches: An ecumenical Christian association dedicated to the search for Christian unity. Member churches promote reconciliation; theological dialogue, renewal of faith, life and witness; and a sharing of resources. Members support each other in evangelism. Founded in 1948. Headquartered in Geneva, Switzerland, with a New York City office. Member churches come from more than 100 countries and most Protestant and Orthodox Christian traditions, including The United Methodist Church. Convenes an international assembly every seven years. Last assembly: 1998 in Harare, Zimbabwe.

World Without War Council: A Berkeley, California-based peace group founded in 1958. Supports and develops programming for nonviolent resolutions to political conflict. Promotes the growth of free societies, strengthening U.S. common civic culture and nurturing nongovernmental organizations.

Works Cited

"AAC Ministry Affiliates & Links." *American Anglican Council* website viewed 25 March 2003 <http://www.americananglican.org/Affiliated/AffiliatedMain.cfm>.

"About Good News." *Good News* website viewed 16 March 2003 <http://www.goodnewsmag.org/hoffice/Index_Hoffice.htm>.

Alliance for Marriage website viewed 29 March 2003 and 8 April 2003 <http://www.allianceformarriage.org>.

___. "Board Of Advisors." <http://www.allianceformarriage.org/board/board.htm>.

___. "Mission Statement and Agenda" <http://www.allianceformarriage.org/mission/mission.htm>.

Asbury College (see "Journalism Department Background." Asbury College, below).

Association for Church Renewal website viewed 8 April 2003 <http://www.ird-renew.org/Issues/IssuesList.cfm?c=20#acr_purpose>.

"Bishop McCleskey Defends Bishop Sprague." *Institute on Religion and Democracy UM Action* website viewed 14 November 2002, 17 March 2003 and 8 April 2003 <http://www.ird renew.org/About/About.cfm?ID=505&c=36>.

Book of Discipline (see The United Methodist Church, below).

Book of Resolutions (see The United Methodist Church, below).

"A Brief History of Affirmation." *Affirmation* website viewed 15 March 2003 and 8 April 2003 <http://www.umaffirm.org/afhistory.html>.

Broadway, Bill. "Evangelicals' Voices Speak Softly About Iraq: Divisions and Precautions Mute Calls For Initiating a War." *Washington Post* 25 January 2003: B9.

Brown, Jim. "Methodist Agency on Warpath Against 'Offensive' Mascots." Agape Press 3 October 2002. Website viewed 26 March 2003 <http://headlines.agapepress.org/archive/10/32002e.asp>. Quoting Mark Tooley, director of UM Action.

Brown, Jim and Jody Brown. "'Good News' Movement Seeks Traditional Biblical Stance within Methodism." Agape Press 3 February 2003. Website viewed 20 March 2003 <http://headlines.agapepress.org/archive/2/32003d.asp>.

___. "Methodist Minister Rebels Against Bishop's Heretical Statements: Conservative Leader Says 'No More' to Undesignated Giving to Local Church." Agape Press 3 October 2002. Website viewed 17 March 2003 and 9 April 2003 <http://headlines.agapepress.org/archive/10/32002a.asp>.

Brown, Ruth. Interview by the author. 18 March 2003.

Caldwell, Gilbert H. Letter to the author. 19 March 2003.

CPER Alert (Californians to Protect Employee Rights). "Birds of A Feather Spend Together." Sacramento, 20 March 1998.

Carroll, Ewing. Interview by the author. 20 March 2003.

Catalyst Online. A project of A Foundation for Theological Education. Website viewed 23 March 2003 and 9 April 2003. <http://www.catalystresources.org>.

Cizik, Richard. Interview by the author. 29 February 2003.

Coalition for United Methodist Accountability. "Coalition Planning Further Action for United Methodist Accountability." The Unofficial Confessing

Movement website viewed 9 April 2003 <http://www.ucmpage.org/news/cuma_complaint2.html>.

___. "Renewal Groups Establish Coalition for United Methodist Accountability." The Confessing Movement website viewed 9 April 2003 <http://www.confessingumc.org/cuma.html>.

Confessing Movement website. Website viewed 23 March 2003 <http://www.confessingumc.org>.

"Confessing Movement Information." *Confessing Movement* website viewed 8 April 2003 <http://www.confessingumc.org/information.htm>.

Congressional Budget Office. "An Analysis of the President's Budgetary Proposals for Fiscal Year 2004: An Interim Report." March 2003. Congressional Budget Office website viewed 20 March 2003 <http://www.cbo.gov/showdoc.cfm?index=4080&sequence=0>.

Council of Bishops of The United Methodist Church. "In The Aftermath of 9-11" (Resolution). "A Pastoral Letter to the Whole Church. November 9, 2001." Website viewed 9 April 2003 <http://www.infoserv.umc.org/faq/bishopsstatements.htm#In%20the%2 0 Aftermath%20of%209-11>.

Cowan, Wayne. "Digesting the Digest." *Christianity and Crisis* 21 March 1983: 55.

Cromartie, Michael and Irving Kristol, Eds. *Disciples and Democracy: Religions Conservatives and the Future of American Politics.* Grand Rapids: Eerdmans, 1995. Based on the December 1993 proceedings of a symposium at the Ethics and Public Policy Center.

"Croning Leads To Complaints-Possible Cover-up Leads To Complainants 'Going Public.'" *Unofficial Confessing Movement* website viewed 22 March 2003 <http://www.UCMPage.org/news/wicca_story6.html>.

Daly, Lewis C. "A Church at Risk: The Episcopal 'Renewal' Movement." *IDS Insights* 22 (2001).

___. "Power and Politics in the Making of Ecclesiastical History." *Church & Society* 92 5 May/June 2002.

Decker, Clyde. Letter to the author.

Dobson, James C. and Gary Bauer. *Children at Risk: The Battle for the Hearts and Minds of Our Kids.* Waco: Word Publishing, 1990.

Dolny, Michael. "Think Tanks Y2K: Progressive Groups Gain, But Right Still Cited Twice as Often." *Extra* July-August 2001. Website viewed 20 March 2003 <http://www.fair.org/extra/0108/think_tanks_y2k.html>.

___. "What's in a Label? Right-Wing Think Tanks Are Often Quoted, Rarely Labeled." *Extra* May-June 1998. Website viewed 20 March 2003 <http://www.fair.org/extra/9805/think-tanks.html>.

DuBose, Steven. Telephone interview by author. 24 March 2003.

Edwards, Marion. "Reflections on Guarding, Transmitting, Teaching, and Proclaiming the Apostolic Faith: An Episcopal Responsibility." An address at the North Carolina Conference to the Bi-Annual Bishops Day Apart October 28, 2002. *North Carolina Annual Conference of The United Methodist Church* website viewed 17 March 2003 <http://www.nccumc.org/EdwardsResponse.htm>.

Faith and Freedom. Institute on Religion and Democracy. Summer 1995.

Field, Scott. Confessing the Faith Conference. Presentations. October 24-25, 2002.

Findlay Jr., James F. *Church People in the Struggle: The National Council of Churches and the Black Freedom Movement, 1950-1970.* New York: Oxford University Press, 1993.

Fineman, Howard. "Bush and God." *Newsweek* 10 March 2003: 22-30.

Foundation News, September/October 1983. Washington D.C.: The Council on Foundations.

A Foundation for Theological Education. IRS Form 990 for fiscal year 2000, as cited by Guidestar (a registered trademark of Philanthropic Research).

Gaddy, C. Welton. *Interfaith Insights* Spring 2000. Website viewed 8 April 2003 <http://www.interfaithinsights.org/00sp/presbyterian.htm>.

General Board of Church and Society of The United Methodist Church. "Statement to the Church on the Terrorist Attacks and the U.S. Response" October 13, 2001. *The General Board of Church and Society, The United*

Methodist Church website viewed 8 April 2003 <http://www.umc-gbcs.org/gbpr126.htm>.

___. "Financial Disclosure Report 2000." *The General Board of Church and Society, The United Methodist Church* website viewed 8 April 2003 <http://www.umc-gbcs.org/gcfa1_financial.pdf>.

___. "A Statement on the Iraq War." *The General Board of Church and Society, The United Methodist Church* website viewed 24 March 2003 and 8 April 2003 <http://www.umc-gbcs.org/news/index.php?newsId=266>. (The statement that GBCS puts at the bottom of their releases/statements: "Only General Conference speaks for the entire denomination. The General Board of Church and Society is the international public policy and social action agency of The United Methodist Church. The board is charged by General Conference....")

___. "The United Methodist Building." *The General Board of Church and Society, The United Methodist Church* website viewed 8 April 2003 <http://www.umc-gbcs.org/75th-book.htm#1>.

General Board of Global Ministries of The United Methodist Church, Women's Division. "Resolution on Terrorist Attacks." October 2001 board meeting.

General Commission on Religion and Race of The United Methodist Church. "GCORR Ministry Functions." *The General Commission on Religion and Race* website viewed 26 March 2003 <http//www.gcrr.org/Original%20Web/ministry.htm>.

General Commission on the Status and Role of Women of The United Methodist Church. "GCSRW: Who We Are." *The General Commission on the Status and Role of Women* website viewed 26 March 2003 <http://gcsrw.org/whoweare>.

Gilbert, Kathy. "Complaints Dismissed Against Bishop Joseph Sprague." United Methodist News Service. 18 February 2003. *UMNS* website viewed 22 March 2003 <http://www.umns.umc.org/03/feb/086.htm>.

___. "Group Files Complaint Against Bishop Sprague." United Methodist News Service. 9 January 2003. *UMNS* website viewed 22 March 2003 <http://www.umns.umc.org/03/jan/011.htm>.

Good News: Home Office Page. *Good News* website viewed 16 March 2003 <http://www.goodnewsmag.org/hoffice/Index_Hoffice.htm>.

Good News IRS Form 990: 1997-1999.

Good News Sample Petitions for General Conference 2004. *Good News* website viewed 19 March 2003 <http://www.goodnewsmag.org/petitions/petitions.html>.

Google Search for "Rev. Mary Kraus." 22 March 2003. *Google* website viewed 22 March 2003 <http://www.google.com/search?hl=en&lr=&ie=ISO-8859-1&q=%22Rev.+Mary+Kraus%22>.

Grant Data Project Page. *Media Transparency* website viewed 20 March 2003 <http://www.mediatransparency.org/search_results/info_on_any_recipient.php?recipientID=175>.

____. *Media Transparency* website viewed 20 March 2003 <http://www.mediatransparency.org/search_results/info_on_any_recipient.php?recipientID=283>.

Greenhouse, Linda. "Can the Justices Buck What Establishment Backs?" *The New York Times*. 30 March 2003: Sec. 4:4.

Gros, Jeffrey. "Which Ecumenism?" *The Christian Century* 11 January 2003: 32-34.

Heidinger II, James V. (Association for Church Renewal chair) "A Brief History." *Institute on Religion and Democracy* website as viewed 7 April 2003 <http://www.ird-renew.org/Issues/IssuesList.cfm?c=20#acr_purpose>.

____. "Are There Any Theological Boundaries?" *Good News* September-October 2002: 11. Website viewed 17 March 2003 <http://www.goodnewsmag.org/magazine/5SeptOct/so02edit.htm>.

____. "Can We Recover Our Doctrinal Heritage?" *Good News* May-June 1997:9.

____. Confessing the Faith Conference. Presentations. October 24-25, 2002.

____. Fund-raising letter for Good News. *Good News*. November 1994.

____. Fund-raising letter for Good News. *Good News*. January 1995.

___. "Good News Board Urges Episcopal Accountability, Laments Action Dissolving Local Church, and Honors Virgil Maybray." Press Release. 14 August 2002. *Good News* website viewed 17 March 2003 <http://www.goodnewsmag.org /news/0802GNBoard.html>.

___. "The History of Renewal in The United Methodist Church," (1997). Website viewed 15 March 2003 <http://www.goodnewsmag.org/renewal/30years.htm/>.

___. "The Role of Gatekeepers." *Good News* November-December 2003. Website viewed 22 March 2003 <http://www.goodnewsmag.org/magazine/6NovDec/nd02edit.htm>.

___. "Time for a Change at the Women's Division." *Good News* March-April 2002.

___. Editorial. *Good News* July-Aug 2000.

Heritage Foundation. Telephone inquiry by author. 25 Feb. 2003.

Hewitt, Don. Interview with Larry King. Larry King Live. CNN. 2 December 2002.

"How General Conference Works." United Methodist News Service *General Conference News* web page viewed 23 March 2003 and 8 April 2003 <http://www.umns.umc.org/gc2000news/pressbook/prbk6.htm>.

Howell, Leon. *Acting in Faith.* Geneva: World Council of Churches, 1982.

___. *Funding the War of Ideas.* Cleveland: United Church of Christ, 1995.

___. "Old Wine, New Bottles: The Institute on Religion and Democracy." *Christianity and Crisis* 21 March 1983: 50.

___. "LeFever at the Edge of Power." *Christianity and Crisis* 2 March 1981: 35.

___. "Religion, Politics, Money and Power." Washington, D.C.: The Interfaith Alliance Foundation, 2001.

Institute for Policy Studies. Telephone interview with author. February 2003.

The Institute for Religion and Democracy. IRS Form 990: 2001.

Ives, Bishop S. Clifton. untitled speech, General Board of Church and Society meeting, March 24, 2001. *General Board of Church and Society, The*

United Methodist Church website viewed 10 April 2003 <www.umc-gbcs.org>.

"The John Wesley Fellowship Program." *Catalyst Online* website viewed 9 April 2003 <http://www.catalystresources.org/fellowship.html>.

"Journalism Department Background." Asbury College website viewed 20 March 2003 and 9 April 2003 <http://www.asbury.edu/dept_sites/academic/com/journal.cfm>.

Kaiser, Robert. "Scaife Denies Ties to 'Conspiracy,' Starr." *Washington Post* 17 December 1998: A2.

Kaiser, Robert and Ira Chinoy. "Scaife: Funding Father of the Right." *Washington Post* 2 May 1999: A1+. Website viewed 20 March 2003 <http://www.washingtonpost.com/wp-srv/politics/special/clinton/stories/scaifemain050299.htm>.

Kell, Carl and Raymond L. Camp. *In the Name of the Father: The Rhetoric of the New Southern Baptist Convention.* Carbondale, Illinois: Southern Illinois University Press, 1999.

Keysor, Charles W. "Confronting the Cults." *Good News* 1974 Winter: 9.

___. "The Gathering Storm." *Good News* 1974 Spring: 19-23.

___. "Here We Go Again #3." *Good News* September-October 1978: 62.

___. "In the Aftermath of Atlanta." *Good News* 1972 Summer: 38, 45.

___. "Leprosy on the Body of Christ." *Good News* 1974 Fall: 56-62.

___. "Methodism's Silent Minority: A Voice for Orthodoxy." Reprinted from *Christian Advocate* 14 July 1966. *Good News* website viewed 15 March 2003 <http://www.goodnewsmag.org/renewal/silent_minority.htm>.

___. "Political Action?" *Good News* January-March 1971: 27.

___. "The Story of Good News" *Good News* April-June 1972: 12-19.

Kilpatrick, Joe. Confessing the Faith Conference. Presentation. October 24, 2002.

Knippers, Diane. "Commentary: Being Anti-Anti War." 27 January 2003. *Institute on Religion and Democracy* website viewed 20 March 2003

<http://www.ird-renew.org/news/NewsPrint.cfm?ID=559&c=4>.

___. "Legislative Team Bears Fruit in Denver." American Anglican Council press release. 29 September 2000. Website viewed 21 March 2003 <http://www.americananglican.org/news/NewsPrint.cfm?ID=45&c=2>.

___. "Special Report from Houston." *Good News* January-February 1978: 5-6.

Kraus, Mary. Interview. March 2003.

Lambrecht, Thomas. Confessing the Faith Conference. Presentation. October 24, 2002.

Larry King Live. (See "Hewitt, Don" above.)

Lewallen, Brad. Telephone interview with author. 4 March 2003.

"Lifewatch and Renew Address Your Concerns in the Abortion Debate." Flyer. No date.

Lifewatch website. Website viewed 23 March 2003 <http://www.lifewatch.org>.

Lind, Michael. *Dissent* (1995 Winter).

Marrs, Texe. Flashpoint/Living Trust Ministries. 1996.

Martin, William. *With God on Our Side: The Rise of the Christian Right in America.* New York: Broadway Books, 1996.

McClain, George. "Apostles of Reaction: A Critical Evaluation of the 'Good News' Leadership." *Social Questions Bulletin* November-December 1978.

McCleskey, J. Lawrence. Letter to the Clergy of the South Carolina Annual Conference and Other Interested Persons. 4 November 2002. *South Carolina Annual Conference of The United Methodist Church* website viewed 17 March 2003 <http://www.umcsc.org/bishop/letterpreface.htm>.

McCutcheon, William. "The Methodist League for Faith and Life," *Explor: A Journal of Theology* 2.2 (Fall 1976) Garrett-Evangelical Theological Seminary: 59-67.

McMullen, Cary. "Methodist Bishops Tactfully Disagree." *The Ledger* (Lakeland, Polk County, Florida) 24 November 2002. Website viewed 17

March 2003 <http://www.theledger.com/apps/pbcs.dll/artikkel?SearchID=
7312914 9828110&Avis=LL&Dato=20021124&Kategori=NEWS&Lopenr
=211240326&Ref= AR>.

Mead, Frank S. *12,000 Religious Quotations.* Grand Rapids: Baker Book
House, 1989: 43.

Miner, Barbara. "The Power and the Money," *Rethinking Schools* 9.3 (1994).

The Mission Society. "Report of Independent Accountant." 31 December
2001, 31 December 2002.

The Mission Society website viewed 23 March 2003 <http://www.msum.org>.

National Committee for Responsive Philanthropy. "$1 Billion For Ideas:
Conservative Think Tanks in the 1990s." 1999 March: 3.

___. "Moving A Public Policy Agenda: The Strategic Philanthropy of
Conservative Foundations." 1997.

National Education Association. "The Real Story Behind Paycheck
Protection-The Hidden Link Between Anti-Public Education Initiatives: An
Anatomy of the Far Right." 1998 September.

Neil, William. "Good News Movement: 1960s and 70s," *Explor: A Journal
of Theology* (1976): 68.

Nelson, Erik. "UM Seminary Official Promotes Homosexuality to Youth."
15 June 2001. *Institute on Religion and Democracy UMAction* website
viewed 23 March 2003 <http://www.ird-renew.org/news/
NewsPrint.cfm?ID=155&c=5>.

The New Revised Standard Version Bible. Division of Christian Education of
the National Council of Churches of Christ in the United States of America.
Nashville: Cokesbury, 1990.

New York Times Archives. Website viewed 21 March 2003
<http://query.nytimes.com/search/query?query=Institute+for+Religion+
and+Democracy&date=full&submit.x=10&submit.y=9>.

The Occult Page. Traditional Catholic Reflections. Website viewed 22 March
2003 <http://www.geocities.com/romcath1/genoccult.html>.

Oden, Thomas C. "How Orthodoxy is Renewing United Methodism." *Good
News* March-April 2003.

___. "The Trust Clause Governing Use of Property in the United Methodist Church: Faithfulness to the connection according to established doctrinal standards." Oklahoma City: The Scriptorium, 2002. *Good News* website viewed 23 March 2003 <http://www.goodnewsmag.org/news/ 122902TrustClause_FULL.htm>.

"Origin and History of Lifewatch." *Lifewatch* website viewed 7 April 2003 <http://lifewatch.org/origin_and_history_of_lifewatch.html>.

Outler, Albert. (ed.) *John Wesley* (See "Wesley, John" below).

Presbyterian Lay Committee, IRS Form 990, 2000.

"Progress Report: Homosexual Ordination Threat Stimulates Reader Response." *Good News* 1975 Winter: 59-63.

Reed, Ralph. Statement at release of the Contract with the American Family. 17 May 1995.

"Reforming America's Churches Project: 2001-2004." Institute on Religion and Democracy.

Regner, Chris. "Bishop Marion Edwards Becomes Second United Methodist Bishop to Criticize Bishop Sprague." 30 October 2002. *Institute on Religion and Democracy UMAction* website viewed 17 March 2003 <http://www/ird-renew.org/About/About.cfm?ID=489&c=36>.

___. "Heterodox Methodist Bishop Criticizes IRD; Orthodox Methodist Bishop Defends Historic Christian Beliefs." 1 October 2002. *Institute on Religion and Democracy UMAction* website viewed 21 March 2003 <http://www.ird-renew.org/About/About.cfm?ID=470&c=36>.

___. "United Methodist Bishop Rejects Christ's Full Deity, Virgin Birth, Physical Resurrection and Atoning Death." 28 August 2002. *Institute on Religion and Democracy UMAction* website viewed 17 March 2003 <http://www.ird-renew.org/About/About.cfm?ID=440&c=36>.

Renew website viewed 23 March 2003 <http://www.renewnetwork.org>.

Robb, Edmund W. and Julia Robb. *Betrayal of the Church: Apostasy and Renewal in the Mainline Denominations.* Wheaton, Illinois: Crossway Books, 1986.

Robb III, Ed. Confessing the Faith Conference. Presentation. October 25, 2002.

Robb, James S. "Good News Founder Charles W. Keysor Dies at 60." *Good News* January-February 1986: 48-49.

Rooney, Raymond. "The Sacred Cow." Agape Press 20 September 2002. Website viewed 17 March 2003 <http://headlines.agapepress.org/archive/9/202002rr.asp>.

"Schedule of Grants, 2001." *John M. Olin Foundation* website viewed 20 March 2003 <http://www.jmof.org/grants/2001a.htm>.

Scott, Don. "Truth or Facts." *United Methodist Reporter* 19 July 2002.

Short, Faye. Renew letter February 2001.

___. Renew letter March 2002.

___. "We Have a Vision." *Renew Newsletter* Winter 2001, Vol. 8, No. 4.

Sider, Ron and Jim Ball. "A Response to Mark Tooley." 20 December 2002. *Institute on Religion and Democracy* website viewed 20 March 2003 <http://www.ird-renew.org/News/News.cfm?ID=537&c=4>.

Simeon-Netto, Uwe. "Faith and Power Profiles: Diane Knippers." United Press International 22 March 2001.

Singleton, John. "At the Roots of Methodism: Wesley Abhorred 'Curse of War'." United Methodist News Service 18 February 2003.

Skinner Keller, Rosemary. *Georgia Harkness: For Such a Time as This.* Nashville: Abingdon, 1992.

Social Principles (see below The United Methodist Church).

Sprague, C. Joseph. *Affirmations of a Dissenter.* Nashville: Abingdon, 2002.

___. "Affirmations of a Dissenter," unpublished speech delivered at Iliff School of Theology, Denver, January 28, 2002.

___. "Dear Ones." Letter following dismissal of complaint. No date given. *Northern Illinois Annual Conference of The United Methodist Church* website viewed 22 March 2003 <http://www.gbgm-umc.org/nillconf/complaint.htm#statement>.

___. "I can't sit by as well-heeled right tries to take over our church." A Bishop's Commentary 18 October 2002. *Northern Illinois Annual Conference of The United Methodist Church* website viewed 22 March 2003 <http://www.gbgm-umc.org/nillconf/coloct02.htm#1018>.

Stallsworth, Paul. "United Methodism Opposes Partial-Birth Abortion: Good News and Sobering News." *Lifewatch:* A quarterly newsletter for United Methodists. September 2000. Website viewed 7 April 2003 <http://lifewatch.org/lifewatch090100.html>.

Stassen, Glen. *Kingdom Ethics: Following Jesus in Contemporary Context.* Grand Rapids: InterVarsity, 2003 January.

Steinfels, Peter. "Baptizing Reaganism." *Christianity and Crisis* 29 March 1982: 80-85.

Thomas, Cal. "Politics and the Pastor." *Washington Times* 23 April 1995.

Tooley, Mark. "Church and Society Rejects War on Terror." 18 October 2001. *Institute on Religion and Democracy UMAction* website viewed 24 March 2003 <http://www.ird-renew.org/About/About.cfm?ID=211&c=5>.

___. "A Crone Bishop." UM Action: Action Briefing. 31 December 1999. *Institute on Religion and Democracy UMAction* website viewed 22 March 2003 <http://www.ird-renew.org/About/About.cfm?ID=110&c=17&Type=s>.

___. "Church Officials Attack Falwell, Defend Muhammad." 29 October 2002. *Institute on Religion and Democracy* website viewed 20 March 2003 <http://www.ird-renew.org/news/NewsPrint.cfm?ID=485&c=4>.

___. "Florida Bishop Defends Orthodox Christianity" *Good News* November-December 2002. *Good News* website viewed 17 March 2003 <http://www.goodnewsmag.org/magazine/6NovDec/nd02news.htm>.

___. "Homosexuals, the Episcopal Bishop and the President's Pastor," Institute on Religion and Democracy press release. 1 December 1995.

___. "Mainline Churches Ever Firmer on Sexual Standards." 21 February 2002. *Institute on Religion and Democracy* website viewed 23 March 2003 <http://www.ird-renew.org/news/NewsPrint.cfm?ID=305&c=3>.

___. "A Methodist Moment in Washington." 31 January 2001. *Institute on Religion and Democracy UMAction* website viewed 9 April 2003

<http://www.ird-renew.org/About/About.cfm?ID=80&c=5>.

___. "The President's Pastor." *Faith and Freedom.* Spring 1995.

___. "Sample Resolution for Shutting Down the United Methodist Lobby Office in Washington, D.C." December 11, 2001. *Institute on Religion and Democracy UMAction* website viewed 9 April 2003 <http://www.ird-renew.org/About/About.cfm?ID=250&c=5&Type=s>.

___. "A Response to Ron Sider and Jim Ball." 20 December 2002. *Institute on Religion and Democracy* website viewed 20 March 2003 <http://www.ird-renew.org/News/News.cfm?ID=538&c=4>.

___. Telephone inquiry by author. 6 March 2003.

___. "UM Bishop Timothy Whitaker Defends Christian Orthodoxy." 24 September 2002. *Institute on Religion and Democracy UMAction* website viewed 17 March 2003 <http://www.ird-renew.org/About/About.cfm?ID= 466&c=36>.

___. "United Methodists Respond to Terror." 25 September 2001. *Institute on Religion and Democracy UMAction* website viewed 24 March 2003 <http://www.ird-renew.org/About/About.cfm?ID=203&c=5>.

___. "What Would Jesus Drive?" 4 December 2002. *Institute on Religion and Democracy* website viewed 20 March 2003 <http://www.ird-renew.org/news/NewsPrint.cfm?ID=514&c=4>.

Transforming Congregations website viewed 7 March 2003 <http://www.transformingcong.org>.

UCMPage.org. United Methodist Accountability Watch (see below, "United Methodist Accountability Watch") and the Unofficial Confessing Movement page.

___. "Croning Leads To Complaints..." (see above, "Croning Leads to Complaints....")

UMAction. "UM Action at General Conference." Institute on Religion and Democracy. Summer 2000: 5-6.

___. "Ecumenical Student Conference Includes Pro-'Gay' Themes." 1 April 1999. *Institute on Religion and Democracy UMAction* website viewed 23 March 2003 <http://www.ird-renew.org/About/About.cfm?ID=113&c=17>.

___. "Pro-'Gay' Mainline Church Caucus Groups Rally." 5 February 2001. *Institute on Religion and Democracy UMAction* website viewed 23 March 2003 <http://www.ird-renew.org/About/About.cfm?ID=79&c=5>.

___. "UM General Conference Rejects Homosexual Agenda." 1 July 2000. *Institute on Religion and Democracy UMAction* website viewed 9 April 2003 <http://www.ird-renew.org/About/About.cfm?ID=109&c=17>.

"UMDecision 2000: Three Things Delegates Can Do." Videotape. The Forum for Scriptural Christianity, Inc. No date.

"UM Finance Agency Declines to Act Against Pro-Homosexuality UM Magazine." 8 March 2001. *Institute on Religion and Democracy UMAction* website viewed 9 April 2003 < http://www.ird-renew.org/About/About.cfm?ID=68&c=5>.

UMNS How General Conference Works (See "How General Conference Works," above).

"United Methodist Accountability Watch." *UCMPage* website viewed 22 March 2003 <http://www.ucmpage.org/news/cuma_account.html>.

The United Methodist Church. *The Book Of Discipline of The United Methodist Church, 2000.* Editor Harriett Jane Olson. Nashville: The United Methodist Publishing House, 2000.

___. *The Book of Discipline of The United Methodist Church,* years 1972, 1976, 1980, 1984, 1988, 1992, 1996. Nashville: The United Methodist Publishing House, 1972, 1976, 1980, 1984, 1988, 1992, 1996.

___. *The Book Of Resolutions of The United Methodist Church, 2000.* Nashville: The United Methodist Publishing House, 2000.

___. *The United Methodist Hymnal — Book Of United Methodist Worship.* Nashville: The United Methodist Publishing House, 1989.

"United Methodists Love Them Both." *Lifewatch.* Flyer. No date.

Waltz, Alan K. *A Dictionary for United Methodists.* Nashville: Abingdon Press, 1991.

Watson, Michael. Editorial. *Wesleyan Christian Advocate* 167. 8 (18 October 2002): 9.

Watson, Philip S. (editor) *The Message of the Wesleys.* Grand Rapids: Zondervan, 1984.

Wesley, John. "Catholic Spirit," Sermon 39, *The Works of John Wesley, Vol. 2, Sermons II, 34-70,* editor Albert C. Outler, (Nashville: Abingdon Press, 1985: 82.) This sermon was also available on the *General Board of Global Ministries* website as viewed on 16 March 2003 <http://gbgm-umc.org/umhistory/wesley/sermons/serm-039.stm>.

___. Explanatory Notes on 1 Peter 4.

___. *Wesley Works* (Jackson edition). Grand Rapids: Baker Book House, 1978.

___. Preface. *Hymns and Sacred Poems.*

___. Doctrine on Original Sin 1762.

___. Sermon 33: Upon Our Lord's Sermon on the Mount (XIII). <http://gbgm-umc.org/UMHistory/Wesley/Sermons/serm-033.stm>.

Whitaker, Timothy. Letter to the Bishops. No date given. Florida Annual Conference of *The United Methodist Church* website viewed 22 March 2003 <http://www.flumc.org/bishop_whitaker/Letter%20to%20the%20Bishops .pdf>.

___. "A Response to Bishop Sprague." No date given. *Florida Annual Conference of The United Methodist Church* website viewed 22 March 2003 <http://www.flumc.org/bishop_whitaker/Response%20to%20Bishop%20 Sprague.pdf>.

White, Jason. "Catholic 'Hawks' Argue Justness of War with Iraq." Religion News Service 10 March 2003.

Wildmon, Donald. "UM Religious Leader Calls for Withhold Financial Support for Heretical Bishop." *The Unofficial Confessing Movement* website viewed 25 February and 17 March 2003 <http://www.ucmpage.org/news/sprague_charges8.html>.

Winkler, Jim. Unpublished paper.

Wogaman, Phil. Interview by author. 8 February 2003.

___. "Playing Hardball on Holy Ground." *Zion's Herald* March-April 2003: 7-8.

Woodson, Leslie H. "Leucocytes in the Body of Christ." *Good News* October-December 1971: 23-28.

Appendix

Institute on Religion and Democracy's Reforming America's Churches Project 2001-2004
Executive Summary

Synopsis: Liberal Theology failed America's mainline churches in the Twentieth Century. Striving to become "relevant," they instead lost millions of church members. These diminished but still influential denominations are now starting to acknowledge their mistakes. Even their leaders are open to new directions. The IRD believes that the next four years offer a rare opportunity to redirect these churches away from their reflexive alliance with the political left and back towards classical Christianity. Conservatives have won surprising victories on key theological and sexuality issues at recent church conventions. Now is the time to translate those victories into real influence for conservatives within the permanent governing structures of these churches, so they can help renew the wider culture of our nation. We will emphasize the importance of ecumenical alliances with social conservative Roman Catholics and Evangelicals.

Market: Over 8.3 million Americans belong to the United Methodist Church, which is America's third largest denomination. Over 3.5 million Americans belong to the Presbyterian Church (USA). And over 2.3 million belong to the Episcopal Church. Although together these churches include just under ten percent of America's total church membership, their influence is disproportionate to their numbers. Their respective memberships include remarkably high numbers of leaders in politics, business, and culture. For example, over one-third of the members of the U.S. Senate belong to these three denominations. These denominations include a disproportionate number of higher income and educated Americans. Every year they collect about $8 billion from their members. Collectively, the institutions of these denominations have billions of dollars in endowments. They are affiliated with hundreds of colleges, universities, seminaries, academies and charitable outreach centers. They include over 50,000 local churches. In short, despite their fallen membership numbers of recent decades, these denominations are still flagship churches that directly or indirectly influence millions of Americans.

To reach them and other members, we disseminate news releases to broadcast media, to every major newspaper religion writer in the country, to every major religious magazine, and to key columnists, for a total of over 1,000 media contacts. We place op-eds exposing the Religious Left on the editorial pages of major newspapers, in religious journals, conservative publications and church renewal media. Our staff regularly speaks on radio talk shows and occasionally on television. IRD's quarterly *Faith and Freedom* journal is sent to over 12,000 supporters, church leaders and media contacts. Our denominational publications now reach 285,000 households and we project growth to 560,000. The combined audiences of reform publications in the Association for Church Renewal total nearly a million households.

Action plan: Our total program for influencing the governing church conventions of three denominations will cost over $3.6 million over the next four years....Target dates are the national church conventions of three major U.S. denominations. The United Methodist Church (April 2004, Pittsburgh), the Presbyterian Church (U.S.A.) (annual, various locations) and the Episcopal Church (July 2003, Minneapolis.)

Grassroots expansion: IRD's three denominational committees are Episcopal Action, United Methodist Action and Presbyterian Action. All three empower conservative church members with reporting about their church structure that they will not otherwise hear. IRD is giving special attention to reform of the United Methodist Church, America's third largest religious body, and the largest denomination under Religious Left control. *UM Action Briefing* currently goes to 275,000 households. Its circulation is expected to be over 500,000 by the start of 2004....

Association for Church Renewal/Next Generation Project: We are a chief organizer of this coalition of conservative/evangelical renewal groups in all the major mainline churches. The association allows us to synchronize strategies across denominational lines and to counteract the influence of liberal ecumenical groups, such as the National and World Councils of Churches. Key to the longer-range success of the church reform movement is recruiting a younger generation of reformers. The IRD has the experience, expertise, connections and vision to recruit and train young church members for this task.

Organizing: We will annually prepare resolutions for local and regional church conventions in the three major denominations. These resolutions will call attention to egregious behavior by radical church leaders and will be important tools for grassroots organizing. They will also focus on positive, proactive initiatives that unite traditional religious believers and discredit the Religious Left. Working with other renewal organizations, we will identify electable conservative candidates for national church conventions. We will help train elected delegates to be effective at church conventions. We also will assist conservatives who serve on the boards of key church agencies so as to have direct influence over the permanent staff.

Evaluation: This project may be judged based on the expansion of IRD's audience as expressed through increased circulation of *Faith and Freedom* and our denominational briefings, through publication of IRD-originated information in secular and religious media outlets, and through passage of our resolutions in regional and national church bodies. Long-range results will be expressed through the election of conservatives and moderates to the boards of church agencies — a more indirect process, but one that is vitally important to long-term reform.

Grantee: The IRD was founded in 1981 to combat the irresponsible political lobbying of mainline churches. Much of IRD's initial focus was upon directly countering the influence of church leaders in religious and secular elite. Our more recent emphasis is upon directly reaching millions of American churchgoers through the media, coalition building and our own publications. Diane Knippers is IRD president....Alan Wisdom is vice president....Mark Tooley directs the United Methodist committee. Together these three leaders represent 46 years of professional reform work.

Bishops' Statement on 9-11:
Council of Bishops Pastoral Letter
November 9, 2001
A Pastoral Letter to the Whole Church

Dear Sisters and Brothers in Christ,

Grace and peace be to you in the name of our Lord, Jesus Christ.

The sad and terrible events in the United States of America, on Sept. 11, 2001, and beyond, compel us to speak words of hope and peace to United Methodist people in the 120 annual conferences in more than 50 countries of the world. Stunned and shattered by terrorist attacks in the United States and the threat of bioterrorism, we, your bishops, call upon the church to join us in seeking solidarity with victimized peoples throughout the world.

Our fervent and constant prayers are for those who grieve because they have lost companions and loved ones; for military chaplains and for those persons who are providing the ministry of presence, comfort, healing and hope; for public servants and countless volunteers who have demonstrated selfless generosity; for all who are redemptively reaching out to those persons who have been erroneously connected to terrorism; for the people who have been placed in harm's way and their loved ones; for President Bush and the leaders of all the nations that they may have wisdom and courage to lead people toward justice and peace. We pray for innocent victims who have experienced injuries, loss and death. We also pray for those who wish to do harm. We pray that violence, terrorism and war will cease. We ask you to join us in prayer.

We are extremely concerned for the thousands of people who live in fear and terror and those displaced by war and poverty. We sincerely believe that every conceivable effort must be used to protect those who are innocent and most vulnerable. We are persuaded that we must use the spiritual and human resources of The United Methodist Church to respond in a loving and caring way. We commend churches around the world for their contribution to the appeal, "Love in the Midst of Tragedy," and all other humanitarian offerings.

We, your bishops, believe that violence in all of its forms and expressions is contrary to God's purpose for the world. Violence creates fear, desperation, hopelessness and instability. We call upon the church to be a community of peace with justice and to support individuals and agencies all over the world who are working for the common good for all of God's children. We also call upon the church to study and work toward alleviating the root causes of poverty and the other social conditions that are exploited by terrorists.

As people of the resurrection, we believe that peace has been achieved in Christ; however, this peace is yet to be fully realized in human relationships. The message of the resurrection is that love is stronger than all the forces of evil. Furthermore, it is only sacrificial love, not war, which can reconcile people to God and to each other. We call upon the church, leaders, nations and individuals around the world to make room for love so that the patterns of our common life might reveal God's justice.

We offer this letter with the wondrous promise of Advent ringing in our ears: "But the angel said to them, 'Do not be afraid; for see I am bringing to you good news of great joy for all the people (Luke 2:10).'"

Peace,
Bishops of The United Methodist Church

http://www.infoserv.umc.org/faq/bishopsstatements.htm#In%20the%20Aftermath%20of%209-11

General Board of Church and Society Statement October 13, 2001
Statement to the Church on the Terrorist Attacks and the U.S. Response

This a statement issued by the General Board of Church and Society at its October board meeting. All United Methodist clergy are urged to share the statement with their congregations.

We the United Methodist General Board of Church and Society (GBCS) join United Methodists and all people around the world as we mourn those who have died, comfort those who have experienced loss and pray together while facing anxious days ahead. In this time of terror and tragedy, we pray to God with humility and with seeking hearts. Our lives have changed, and for those of us who live in the United States, our sense of invulnerability and invincibility has been destroyed. We rejoice that as children of God we need not fear God nor seek to appease God. We are trustful and open to the God of love.

We claim the teachings of the Prince of Peace who instructs us to love and pray for our enemies and refrain from responding to violence with violence. As we join people around the world in our resolve to bring terrorists to justice, we understand that war is not an appropriate means of responding to criminal acts against humanity.

We reaffirm The United Methodist resolution on Terrorism which states, "we oppose the use of indiscriminate military force to combat terrorism, especially where the use of such force results in casualties among noncombatant citizens who are not themselves perpetrators of terrorist acts....We condemn all acts of terrorism, with no exception for the target or the source. (*The Book of Resolutions of The United Methodist Church, 2000,* page 787.) We urge that food aid be provided to refugees in Afghanistan and other countries through established humanitarian channels distinct from military action. Furthermore, we urge the United States and the international community to provide protection for refugees, and to make plans now for the eventual rehabilitation of refugees and the establishment of a stable and just Afghan society.

In our limited human vision, we turn to God for guidance. In our mourning, we pray for God's comfort. In our hunger and thirst for righteousness, we seek God's forgiveness for our self-righteousness. As Matthew 5:9 reminds us, Jesus calls the children of God to be peacemakers. We live with the uncertainty of these times seeking divine patience and strength. We look to God to lead us to the greater good — love combined with justice and truth aligned with trust. We embrace with confidence a faith that seeks God's purposes.

In these tense days, the Church is called to be an instrument of service, healing, and peace. Toward this end, we call upon United Methodist congregations to:

a) Be in a season of prayer for peace, for all who suffer and mourn, for those who serve, especially those in harm's way, and for courage to respond to God's guidance;

b) Become bridge-builders in your community between Christians and persons of other religious faiths through education and outreach;

c) Offer acts of hospitality to Arabs, Muslims and all others in your community who may suffer at this time from acts of hatred and prejudice;

d) Reflect upon what our Church has declared — that war is incompatible with the teachings and example of Christ (Social Principles, ¶165 VI(C));

e) Inform young people in your congregation that we extend our ministry to those who choose to serve in the military or those who choose not to serve. Inform those who choose not to serve in the military of the option to register as a conscientious objector in the U.S. and other countries where the option is available (Social Principles, ¶164 V (G));

f) Study the root causes of terrorism, the history of Western involvement in the Middle East, and work to end terrorism;

g) Call and visit your government officials to urge an end to all violence and war and to use the United Nations as a primary venue for multilateral action. Ask them also to support the establishment of the International Criminal Court that would allow nations to bring to trial perpetrators of criminal acts against humanity, and urge President Bush to submit to the Senate for ratification the Treaty creating the Court (Social Principles, ¶164 VI (D));

h) Continue with generous support and donations to UMCOR for Afghanistan refugees and the victims of the attacks in the U.S.

It is our firm belief that military actions will not end terrorism. As people called to be a visible sign of God's ever-present love, we know that violence will not bring God's peace. We are grateful for those efforts by President Bush and the U.S. Congress toward a measured response to September 11. We continue to say no to war and encourage our leaders to respond cautiously. "Let us not compound a grievous tragedy with a grievous error."

Only the General Conference speaks for the entire United Methodist Church. The United Methodist General Board of Church and Society of the Church is the denomination's international public policy and social action agency.

http://www.umc-gbcs.org/gbpr126.htm

Women's Division Statement
October 2001

The terrorist attacks on the United States on September 11 have deeply affected us as individuals, as a nation, and as people of faith. Our prayers and concerns go out to the families of many faiths and many countries affected by the tragedy.

As followers of Jesus Christ, we are called to choose life over death (Deuteronomy 30:19). We are also called to love our enemies and pray for those who persecute us (Matthew 5:44). As United Methodist Women, we are challenged to commit ourselves, through prayer, study and action, to continue the search for peace with justice.

We therefore call on United Methodist Women to:

A) Urge the President to use diplomatic means to bring the perpetrators of terrorist acts to justice and to end the bombing of Afghanistan. Countries of the South as well as the North must be involved as decision makers in addressing efforts to combat terrorism.

B) Reach out to persons of other faiths and become educated on the beliefs of Islam. We commend as a resource the 1989-1990 mission study on the World of Islam and the November 2000 issue of *Response* on "Interfaith Challenges, Interfaith Understanding." (See *Book of Resolutions, 2000* "Called to Be Neighbors and Witnesses: Guidelines for Interreligious Relationships.")

C) Work to prevent racial profiling and acts of harassment or violence directed at Muslims, Arabs, and those perceived to be Muslims. (See the *Book of Resolutions, 2000* "Prejudice Against Muslims and Arabs in the United States.") Further, we ask our members to continue to monitor hate-crime activity and to report such incidents to the Women's Division.

D) Urge the President to press for peace in the Middle East, including security for the state of Israel and justice and sovereignty for the Palestinian people.

E) Become informed on proposed anti-terrorist legislation through the UMW Action Network and the *Legislative Letter* and oppose efforts to curb constitutionally protected civil liberties.

Index